In
Step
with
the
Spirit

In Step with the Spirit

A STUDY OF THE FRUIT OF THE SPIRIT
GALATIANS 5:22-23

RUBEL SHELLY

BAKER BOOK HOUSE
Grand Rapids, Michigan 49516

ISBN: 0-8010-8276-5

Second printing, January 1988

Printed in the United States of America

Contents

Introduction

For some time I had been reflecting on a book about the fruit of the Spirit; yet, when I turned to the task, I learned to my dismay (and some embarrassment) that my resource files contained very little on the subject. Oh, yes, there was quite a bit of material on the various *works of the flesh*, but there were no folders labeled FRUIT OF THE SPIRIT. *Why*, I wondered, *was this so?*

Surely it reflected my sinful nature, a tendency to concentrate on fighting evil rather than promoting good. Oh, there *is* a time to warn and rebuke and identify evil things, but the Bible is balanced in favor of the positive, which will fill us with goodness and crowd out the desire for sin.

Light cancels darkness. And if we will allow God to fill our lives with the fruit of his Holy Spirit, we will no longer live or walk in darkness.

And what is true of an individual's experience is also true of the church. We are too program-oriented rather than Spirit-oriented. The late Dr. A. W. Tozer once said, "If the Holy Spirit was withdrawn from the church today, 95 percent of what we do would go on and no one would know the difference. If the Holy Spirit had been withdrawn from the New Testament church, 95 percent of what they did would stop, and everybody would know the difference."

In Galatians 5:22, 23, Paul lists various facets of Christian virtue and character. He refers to them collectively as the *fruit* (singular) *of the Spirit.* This is a fragrant bouquet of graces. The flowers are not separable for giving one at a time. They form a bouquet, and each one possesses its own particular hue and fragrance. *Love, joy, peace, patience, kindness, goodness, faithfulness, gentleness,* and *self-control*—these divine qualities grow simultaneously in the life of someone in whom the Spirit of God dwells, not singly or in isolation from one another.

It is my prayer that you will find encouragement in this book to keep in step with the Spirit, allowing him to produce his beauty in your life.

Rubel Shelly

1

Moved by a New Spirit

It borders on a lie for some orthodox Christians to confess a trinitarian view of deity. We say that we believe in God the Father, God the Son, and God the Holy Spirit. Yet for too many of us during our experience as children of God the Holy Spirit has been what D. Stuart Briscoe has in *Let's Get Moving* called the "silent partner in the godhead."

We don't really know him in the way we know the Father and the Son. Some of us would more nearly be *bi*nitarians rather than *tri*nitarians. We believe in God the Father. We believe in God the Son. But we are sometimes more than a little confused about the possibility of knowing God the Holy Spirit.

This is a partial explanation for the charismatic movement of recent times. Against the background of a great dearth of awareness concerning this third member of the godhead, some people discovered the truth of the presence of God's Holy Spirit among men. This caused some of them to embrace excesses, extremes, and even false teachings about that newly discovered member of the godhead. Some of them became, for all practical purposes, pneumatic *uni*tarians. They lost sight of the Father and the Son as they gave almost exclusive focus to the Holy Spirit and the possibility of special gifts at his hand.

9

There are *three* who are God: God the Father, God the Son, and God the Holy Spirit.

Confusion Comes Easily

Perhaps it sounds heretical to say it, but I think it is rather easy to be confused about the Holy Spirit. For one thing, it is harder for most of us to think of the Holy Spirit as a "him" than an "it." The Bible teaches that he is as personal as Father and Son are personal, but one has to work at it to keep that truth fixed in consciousness.

> There does not seem to be much difficulty in thinking of God the Father as personal. The very idea implicit in the word "Father" ensures that we regard Him as a Person in the very fullest sense of that term. . . .
>
> If anything, it is even easier to think of the Son in a personal way. He is the Baby of Bethlehem, the Carpenter of Nazareth, the Teacher of Galilee. . . .
>
> But it is different with the Spirit. "Spirit" is not such an aggressively personal word as "Father." The Spirit has not become incarnate like the Son. We find it hard to picture him. His workings are for the most part inward and secret, we might almost say mystical. He gives us grace, guidance, strength and the like, which we might easily ascribe to a force or influence proceeding from the Father. In the English language, as also in Greek, "Spirit" is a neuter noun, and we find it easier to think of neuters as things than as people. When the New Testament writers want to speak of the Spirit the symbols they use, oil, fire and the like, are usually such as might readily be interpreted of an inanimate force or influence. (Leon Morris. *Spirit of the Living God.* Chicago: Inter-Varsity Press, 1960, p. 34).

Somehow we must begin, not only to make place for all three members of the godhead, but also to see the Holy Spirit in as intensely personal a way as we see the Father and the Son. We must come to realize that our covenantal relationship with God puts us in contact with the Holy Spirit as well as the Father and Son.

The natural confusion which can be generated about the Spirit's essence is compounded by false teaching. Jehovah's Witnesses insist that "the holy spirit" (lower-case letters are always used in their literature) is nothing more than "Jehovah's Active Force," which is used as the instrument of divine accomplishment among men (*"Make Sure of All Things . . .",* Brooklyn: Watchtower Bible and Tract Society of New York, Inc., 1965, p. 466). Very similar to this is the view of the Unitarians, who hold that the Holy Spirit is nothing more than the eternal energy of God.

Sometimes the popular literature or research books people consult when they want some insight into the work of the "silent partner" in the godhead are more harm than help. Some of them grant that a personal Spirit of God exists, and once had contact with men, but insist that his relationship now is less than personal and limited to a "representative indwelling" of believers through the Word of God.

Sometimes when the truth of the personal Spirit of God is discovered, the focus is all wrong. Instead of wanting the real gift of God's Spirit in our daily lives for the purpose it was given, people want special gifts and endowments that will somehow make them into super-Christians instantly and give them access to miraculous powers (*see* Acts 8:18, 19).

What Is the Spirit's Function?

The role of the Holy Spirit is character formation in Christians. The Spirit of God has been given to saved people to make us Christ-like. His role is not to make us do bizarre things, but Christ-like things, in terms of the personalities, dispositions, words, and deeds that flow from us.

The Spirit teaches of Christ through the gospel and brings us to a knowledge of Christ, which permits us to be saved by faith in him. "Faith comes by hearing the message, and the message is heard through the word of Christ" (Rom. 10:17). Even so, the Word of God is made powerful by virtue of the Holy Spirit of God. The spoken or written Word is the "sword" which the Spirit of God uses to convict hearts, lay us bare to the truth about our condition as sinners, and impress us with what heaven has done to save us.

It is the Spirit who renews life within the sinner who has learned of Christ and come to him for salvation. The new birth of John 3 is a birth "of water and the Spirit" (v. 5). The one birth experience has two elements. Water is a material substance and the element which touches our physical bodies in being immersed in Jesus' name; the Spirit of God is the immaterial and spiritual element who touches our spiritual beings. It is the Spirit who quickens and refreshes, not the water. In a Pauline reference to the new birth, the apostle associated the same two elements when he spoke of God's saving men through "the washing of rebirth and renewal by the Holy Spirit, whom he poured out on us generously through Jesus Christ our Savior, so that, having been justified by his grace, we might become heirs having the hope of eternal life" (Titus 3:5b-7).

After the apostolic sermon on Pentecost Day, when the church was founded, people whose hearts were convicted of sin asked what they could do to be saved by the Christ they had earlier rejected and crucified. Peter's answer came back: "Repent and be baptized, every one of you, in the name of Jesus Christ so that your sins may be forgiven. *And you will receive the gift of the Holy Spirit*" (Acts 2:38, italics added).

The Spirit of God is active in giving the enlightening and revealing Word that points to Christ. In the experience of new birth, the Spirit of God is the divine agent of grace to quicken and make alive. At that point of spiritual birth into the family of God, the Spirit is given to indwell us so that our bodies, according to Paul, become actual temples where the Spirit dwells (1 Cor. 6:19, 20; *see also* Gal. 4:6).

Now to this point, most of us are still together. We understand that salvation is by grace, that it is the gift of God, and that the powerful agent who imparts new life is the Holy Spirit. Why does our theology of the Holy Spirit end here?

Is the new life which has been begun in the power of the Spirit now to be lived by law keeping in the strength of the flesh?

Be honest. Do you ever get frustrated in your Christian life? Has any of the joy and excitement you sensed in the beginning, as the Spirit of God led you to see Christ lifted up for your sins, faded with the passing of time? Some believers sadly admit this has been their experience.

It isn't supposed to work that way. Life in Christ is supposed to get better—not flatter—as time goes by. The high point ought not to be left behind when you first come to know him. The high point is "a rich welcome into the eternal kingdom of our Lord and Savior Jesus Christ" (2 Peter 1:11), the end of a gradual coming closer to God in this life through the working of the Spirit of God in your heart and life.

The "high point" of my life on earth hasn't come yet. I am not where I plan to be before I see the Lord's face. Yet the high point for some Christians in all their spiritual experience has been their conversion. Since that time, the excitement and thrill of coming to Christ have turned into dull monotony. The reason is that they have not yet understood that the new life we live in Christ is a life focused more on *being* than *doing*. Being God's yielded vessel in whom the Spirit of God can really live to bear fruit is what matters, not doing all the things we have come up with in our self-help manuals as crucial for proving we are genuine Christians in the strength of the flesh.

If the Spirit of God is in your heart and lives within you, a yielded, surrendered vessel, the things your life displays will allow everyone to know you are God's own. The Spirit of God will bear his fruit in you. Sometimes, though, we want to prove we are Christians, not by the power of the Spirit, but in the strength of our flesh. So we work out codes and draw up checklists. We work out devotional programs or evangelistic strategies that we think will prove to us (and others and God) who we really are. Then we get frustrated and fail because we have been trying to live a spiritual life in the strength of the flesh. It just won't work.

Listen to Paul: "But now, by dying to what once bound us, we have been released from the law so that we serve in the new way of the Spirit, and not in the old way of the written code" (Rom. 7:6). There is Paul's statement of what the few paragraphs above have tried to communicate.

Under the New Testament it's all different. It's not conformity, it's a relationship with a Person. It's not my failure, it's His success. It's not me working for God, it's God working through me. It's not service under the "oldness of the letter," it's service in "newness of the Spirit." Not the letter but the Spirit. Not death but life. Not I but Christ. Not trying but trusting. . . .

It's a whole new ball game. And it cannot be played by the old rules (Robert C. Girard. *Brethren, Hang Loose.* Grand Rapids: Zondervan Publishing House, 1972, pp. 110, 111).

The idea a lot of people have had about religion holds that it is a matter of finding all the rules and living up to them (that is, "the old way of the written code"). That is the way some Jews treated their Old Testament revelation from God. It is the way some Christians treat our New Testament revelation from God. This approach always frustrates the people who try it and winds up making them despise rather than revel in their spiritual lives. The apostle to the Gentiles said there was a better way. He called it service to God "in the new way of the Spirit" (Rom. 7:6, italics added).

Christianity can be a frustrating walk on a dead-end street. For the person who is trying to live a new life by old rules (which say success is in finding a five- or ten-step ladder to glory, and climbing it rung by rung in your own strength, self-determination, and discipline), Christianity is a heavy burden and often not worth the effort. That is the old way of the written code.

In both Romans and Galatians, Paul discusses this old way and describes it as "justification by works." The new way is the way of the Spirit where the key is not doing but being. God gives his Spirit for the specific purpose of making us what we know we need to be and what, because we have experienced cleansing in the blood of Jesus, we really want to be. But the power to bring it about is in the Spirit of God rather than in our strength.

It is time we developed a theology of Christian living which includes the previously silent partner of the godhead. We must study and try to understand the role he plays in the process of sanctification. We must not grieve or quench the Holy Spirit. We must yield to him, so God's fruitful Spirit can get on with his business in our lives and transform us by his power.

A New Approach to Holiness

In Galatians 5, Paul writes at some length about life in this "new way" of the Spirit. Let's examine what he says section by section.

You, my brothers, were called to be free. But do not use your freedom to indulge the sinful nature; rather, serve one another in love. The entire law is summed up in a single command: "Love your neighbor as yourself." If you keep on biting and devouring each other, watch out or you will be destroyed by each other.

So I say, live by the Spirit, and you will not gratify the desires of the sinful nature. For the sinful nature desires what is contrary to the Spirit, and the Spirit what is contrary to the sinful nature. They are in conflict with each other, so that you do not do what you want. But if you are led by the Spirit, you are not under law (vv. 13–18).

Romans and Galatians deal with the same theme. Both epistles are about justification by faith in Christ. Romans is the full-length version; Galatians is the "Reader's Digest Condensed Version."

The specific context for the writing of Galatians has to do with some false teachers who had gone among new Christians peddling their old Jewish works-righteousness system. They taught that righteousness (that is, right-standing with God) consisted of knowing all the commands and keeping them. So they told the new converts to Christ that they would have to be circumcised, avoid certain foods, keep identifiable holy days, and so forth. Through the reports which had come to him, Paul learned that the work he had started by the Spirit of God among those people of Galatia was being reduced to the level of flesh and lawkeeping.

So Paul wrote the Book of Galatians in a state of holy horror. He warned of the false teachers who were bringing in a "different gospel" (1:6) and "trying to pervert the gospel of Christ" (v. 7). He chided the Galatian converts for being "foolish" in allowing the false teachers to mislead them. He wrote: "I would like to learn just one thing from you: Did you receive the Spirit by observing the law, or by believing what you heard? Are you so foolish? *After beginning with the Spirit, are you now trying to attain your goal by human effort?*" (3:2, 3, italics added).

This whole business of turning from the renewal of God's Spirit to a life based on human effort sounds a bit familiar, doesn't it? Paul said such an approach to the gospel was "really no gospel at all" (v. 1:7a). How right that is! There is no "good news" in the idea that righteousness is by human effort, because all of us tried that method even before we were Christians. We turned over our "new leaves," made resolutions, summoned up all our willpower to struggle with some problem—and fell flat on our faces for all our trouble.

We have tried by the power of flesh and failed before we knew Christ. What difference will it make if, after knowing Christ, we keep fighting by the same old rules? Paul says we were "called to be free"—free from guilt, free from condemnation, and free from the foolish notion that righteousness comes through human effort.

Now it is dangerous to make that statement, and Paul saw the danger in doing so. It can be misunderstood by sincere people. And it can certainly be twisted and perverted by those who are less than sincere. So the apostle covers his flank by warning against misunderstanding or misinterpretation. He says: Your freedom is not indulgence.

"Freedom" doesn't mean that Christians can do anything we want to do. Specifically, freedom is not a license to indulge our "sinful nature." To understand what Paul said about grace and liberation from rule keeping to mean indulgence would be perverting his meaning altogether. How so? The person who has been saved and who is now yielded to the Spirit of God cannot live a self-indulgent life because the power at work in him leads to another end. He will live a righteous and holy life that corresponds to the things he always knew were right. Oh, yes. He has known all along what was right and what was wrong, for he knew the law of God. But now he has a relationship with the empowering Spirit of God, which enables him to keep the law he has always known.

The ability to observe the will of God, the ability to be an obedient child of God, does not come simply from knowing the rules and feeling unworthy before the magnificent Creator of the universe. The power to live up to things that God has told you are right must come from an internal dynamic that is greater than anything in you by virtue of your human nature. That power is going to have to come from a source that is matched to the revelation. If the revelation has been given by the Spirit of God and if that same revealing Spirit is in you to empower you, you can do it. You will have success, not because you are a great rulekeeper, but because you are a yielded vessel to the same Holy Spirit who has revealed the truth to you. Your nature and that revelation are no longer at odds, for your nature has been yielded to the Spirit who has shown you what is holy and right.

The Spirit vs. the Sinful Nature

To understand what Paul is driving at in Galatians 5, you must get hold of the contrast between "flesh" and "Spirit" (KJV, ASV) or "sinful nature" and "Spirit" (NIV).

"Flesh" (Gk, *sarx*) is a word that originally meant the soft, fleshy part of a human being. It soon came to mean the body as a whole, the material part of a person; so by extension the whole man, as conditioned by living in a body of flesh, was denoted by the term. *Sarx* is whatever it is to be in the flesh; it is to be mannish, to be human, to be mortal.

As this word was taken into the Christian vocabulary, and especially by Paul, it came to mean something more significant still. *Sarx* came to denote man as stained with and dominated by sin. It is not that the body is evil, mind you, or even that its natural desires are wicked. It is simply that man too often satisfies his desires in wicked ways which defy his God. For example, the desire for food is innocent. But some want that desire satisfied in a quick, easy way rather than by the slow, hard way of working. So they steal. Or maybe the natural desire is for sexual fulfillment. The desire is good and holy, but to satisfy that desire in homosexual acts or fornication is sinful.

In the New Testament, then, *sarx* can refer not only to the material substance, which is one's body, but to everything evil that man is and is capable of being, apart from God. As Paul uses it here, it is synonymous with "the old man" he talks about so often in his writings. It is that old, pre-Christian man whose heart is focused on the wrong things and who is giving himself over to wicked desires.

Because the word carries all this meaning for the Spirit-guided apostle, our English word *flesh* is probably not the best way to translate it. To the person lacking theological expertise, this word *flesh* just means the stuff we're made of (such as skin, muscles, tendons, and so forth). By reading Paul, he could conclude—as some have—that there is something inherently

evil about the material part of him which is his body. No! Paul
taught no such thing.

What is evil about me is not my bones, cells, and tissues;
it is my *nature* (that is, my sinful propensities, my sinful habits,
what I have learned to do to gratify my desires that are opposed
to God) as a man who walks his own self-willed way rather than
the Spirit's way.

> The flesh is man as he has allowed himself to become in contrast
> with man as God meant him to be. The flesh stands for the total
> effect upon man of his own sin and the sin of his fathers and
> of the sin of all men who have gone before him. The flesh is
> human nature as it has become through sin. Man's sin, his own
> sin and the sin of mankind, has, as it were, made him vulnerable
> to sin. It has made him fall even when he knew he was falling
> and even when he did not want to fall. It has made him such
> that he can neither avoid the fascination of sin nor resist the
> power of sin. The flesh stands for human nature weakened, vitiated,
> tainted by sin. The flesh is man as he is apart from Jesus Christ
> and his Spirit (William Barclay. *Flesh and Spirit: An Examination
> of Galatians 5. 19–23.* Nashville: Abingdon Press, 1962, p. 22).

This "sinful nature" is not innate to me. I was not born with
it and did not receive it genetically. It is something I learned,
practiced, and cultivated over years of living as a sinner. It is
the habit and custom of living the way most of us do, satisfying
the desires that we have in ways that we know offend God.

That is why it thrilled Paul to be able to tell his readers: You
are free from the old things. You are free from sin's guilt and
free from the wrong-headed notion that right-standing with God
is earned through lawkeeping. But he cautioned them against
thinking this gave them permission to indulge their sinful nature.
To the contrary: "Live by the Spirit, and you will not gratify
the desires of the sinful nature" (Gal. 5:16). One will not keep
living in a way that is in opposition to God if he is indwelt
by the divine Spirit, which is his access into all things holy.

"Spirit" (Gk, *pneuma*) originally meant air or wind or breath.
Later it came to refer to that nonmaterial and incorporeal part

of man that leaves him, like his breath, when he dies. Again, however, it was picked up by Christians and adapted to refer both to that nonmaterial human spirit which indwells and activates us and to God's indwelling and activating Holy Spirit. He is nonmaterial and incorporeal in nature; he indwells us for the purpose of developing a Christian character in us.

By virtue of the fact that one belongs to Christ, the Spirit of God is in him. But his sinful nature is still there, too. The old habits and learned responses which are evil have not been obliterated by the fact that he has become a child of God. The sinful nature is still there and resists expulsion. One who tries to deal with that sinful nature in the strength of his own resources is no better equipped for the fight now than he was before becoming a Christian.

Willpower and self-discipline cannot conquer one's sinful nature. If he is to overcome it, it will have to be done by the Spirit of God. That's what Paul said. The sinful nature wants what is contrary to the Spirit; the Spirit wants what is contrary to the sinful nature. "They are in conflict with each other, so that you do not do what you want" (Gal. 5:17b). I can testify to that. I have done things I didn't want to do and was conscious at the time that I was gratifying a desire by doing something that offended my God. I have done that even since becoming a Christian. Someone may be thinking that I was not truly converted and am not a Christian since those things have happened in my life. But I take comfort in the fact that Paul confessed the same thing.

Paul was no prouder of his post-conversion failures than I am of mine. He said that he had resolved not to do certain things only to turn right around and do them; he had resolved to do certain holy things only to lose his resolve and fail (see Rom. 7:14-20). "So I find this law at work: When I want to do good, evil is right there with me. For in my inner being I delight in God's law; but I see another law at work in the members of my body, waging war against the law of my mind and making me a prisoner of the law of sin at work within my members. What a wretched man I am!" (vv. 21-24a).

Life by the Spirit is neither license nor legalism. It is life by a totally new means.

The Enemy Within

As God's Spirit lives in us and works within us, the sinful nature resists. The old man fights back. When we died with Christ and offered the sinful old man to be crucified with him, we renounced the sinful nature. But the dead man won't lie down! He wants the place of dominance in our lives that he had before the Spirit of God took control. So he tries to regain control by seducing us again into the lifestyle which will grieve and quench the Spirit of God.

The acts of the sinful nature are obvious: sexual immorality, impurity and debauchery; idolatry and witchcraft; hatred, discord, jealousy, fits of rage, selfish ambition, dissensions, factions and envy; drunkenness, orgies, and the like. I warn you, as I did before, that those who live like this will not inherit the kingdom of God (Gal. 5:19-21).

James 1:13-15 explains that temptations to do evil do not come from God. We are tempted when our own desires motivate us to satisfy our yearnings by means of wicked acts. "Each one is tempted when, by his own evil desire, he is dragged away and enticed. Then, after desire has conceived, it gives birth to sin; and sin, when it is full-grown, gives birth to death" (vv. 14, 15).

"But I just can't stop doing some of the things Paul lists," you say. "I'm hooked—on alcohol, drugs, sex. . . ."

I won't argue the point with you. You are right. You *cannot* stop! You don't have enough strength to break habits which have become larger than your will. In order to resist sin, you will have to have some power greater than your determination and willpower.

Remember the old fable about the tar baby? The tar baby is a treacherous trap. If you try to give it a good punch, you find out the hand you use to punch or slap it will stick to it. So what is the natural thing to do? Take the other hand and try to pull away. And now you have two hands stuck. So you put a foot against it to push it away and free your hands, and then you are stuck at three points. Before long, the tar baby you were going to beat to a pulp has you within its power. The harder you fight against it, the more trapped you are by it. That is exactly what it is to try to live a Christian life in the powers of the flesh.

The more you try to fight sin and your sinful nature with the resources of your unaided human willpower and strength, the more tied up you are with everything you hate. The "tar baby" of sin gets a firmer hold on you with every self-motivated punch you throw at it. You are bound most tightly of all by your own pride. You will never learn the liberating truth of life by the new way of the Spirit if you don't feel you need it. Set out to live the new life in Christ and be righteous because *you* are smart, *you* are tough, *you* are resourceful—and you will fail utterly and miserably. But if God's Spirit lives in you, that which you could never do in the power of your own resources happens naturally.

God's Spirit Is Fruitful

After listing the "*acts* of the flesh," Paul turns to the "*fruit* of the Spirit." The very terminology may be meaningful. "Acts" are that which you can do acting on your own impulses; "fruit" sounds more like a passive element that happens as the result of something God does within you. If you do it of your resources and activity, there is no glory to God in it. But if God causes it to happen in you, the glory is his. The flesh acts; the Spirit bears fruit.

The fruit of the Spirit signifies a totally different way of life for an individual. It certainly isn't a life of license and abandon. It is a life of holiness, temperance, and beauty.

> But the fruit of the Spirit is love, joy, peace, patience, kindness, goodness, faithfulness, gentleness and self-control. Against such things there is no law. Those who belong to Christ Jesus have crucified the sinful nature with its passions and desires. Since we live by the Spirit, let us keep in step with the Spirit. Let us not become conceited, provoking and envying each other (Gal. 5:22–25).

The proof of God's presence and of his Spirit in your life is not gifts or gab, not special, miraculous powers or great confessions. The proof is a transformed nature. And the key is *being*, not doing.

Do you remember the long conversation Jesus had with his disciples before he went to Jerusalem and the cross? He told them he was going away but the Holy Spirit was coming. "I will ask the Father," he said, "and he will give you another Counselor to be with you forever—the Spirit of truth. The world cannot accept him, because it neither sees him nor knows him. But you know him, for he lives with you and will be in you" (John 14:16, 17).

Why was the Spirit to be given? What would he do on his arrival? He accomplished much, of course. Some of these actions were miraculous in nature. Some centered on the ministry of the apostles, but the more important and permanent of his works *is still in progress*. It is the work of *fruit bearing* in the lives of disciples.

Jesus continued his promise about the coming of the Spirit and said: "I am the vine; you are the branches. If a man remains in me and I in him, he will bear much fruit; apart from me you can do nothing" (John 15:5). Practically anything can be faked—even miracles and signs (*see* 2 Thess. 2:9). The one facet that cannot be faked is Christian temperament, personality, and character. This is the special fruit borne in the life of one who is in Christ and who, by the presence of the indwelling Spirit, has Christ in him.

Christ has chosen us to bear fruit to his glory. "You did not choose me," he reminds us, "but I chose you to go and bear fruit—fruit that will last" (John 15:16a). The choice was made by him. The power is provided by him. The glory belongs to him. Fruitfulness in the power of the Spirit of God is grace-based, not works-based.

Conclusion

Do you ever get discouraged about the lack of growth, power, fellowship, and soul-winning in your life? How are you going to solve the problem?

If you plan to work up a schedule, lay down a regimen, measure up to someone else's expectations, follow what worked for a friend—you are setting yourself up to fail again. You are trying to perform a spiritual act in the powers of the flesh. There is a better way.

The new and better way is to surrender to the Spirit of God. Then the experiences you have never been able to encounter, that you have never been able to live long-term, will become realities. Like fruit on a tree, they will appear as little buds and begin to grow. They will ripen with age. Then, as you get older, instead of becoming bitter and cynical, you will become sweeter and more fruitful in the realness of the Spirit of God.

Who are Christians? Christians are people moved by a *new Spirit*. Not the spirit of this age, not the spirit of our sinful natures, but the Spirit of God who lives in us.

How we can cooperate with God's Spirit to allow our lives to bear beautiful fruit to his glory is what this book is about.

2
Christians Are "Under the Influence"

In a short paragraph from Paul, there appears to be a deliberate play on words with the idea of a person being "filled with" one of two elements, either *wine* or *the Spirit of God.*

> Be very careful, then, how you live—not as unwise but as wise, making the most of every opportunity, because the days are evil. Therefore do not be foolish, but understand what the LORD'S will is. Do not get drunk on wine, which leads to debauchery. Instead, be filled with the Spirit. Speak to one another with psalms, hymns and spiritual songs. Sing and make music in your heart to the LORD, always giving thanks to God the Father for everything, in the name of our LORD Jesus Christ (Eph. 5:15–20).

When a person is, as we euphemistically put it, "under the influence" of alcohol, he acts crazy. The craziness exhibits itself in different forms. Alcohol makes some people sullen, silent, and withdrawn. It makes other people giddy, foolish, and loud. Between these two extremes are all shades and variations of erratic behavior for the person who has come "under the influence."

For one who is "under the influence"—not of wine but of the
Spirit of Christ—his behavior changes, too. He doesn't become
crazy, though. He becomes Christ-like.

When the Spirit Is Controlling You

To the degree that anyone is filled with the Spirit of God,
he serves the Lord—in different ways, perhaps, from another
brother filled with the same Spirit, but always to the single goal
of glorifying God. Just as alcohol causes different people to react
in different ways, so the presence of the Spirit of God causes
different people to pursue different ministries.

The mistake some people make in writing and speaking about
Christian sanctification is to insist: "If the Spirit of God is in
you, you'll have my interests and do what I'm good at doing and
be like me. The twenty-two-step program to this end, which I've
worked out for you, can be purchased in the foyer as you leave."

No, the Spirit of God does not produce the same ministry
and the same expressions of service in the life of each individual.
"There are different kinds of gifts, but the same Spirit. There
are different kinds of service, but the same Lord. There are
different kinds of working, but the same God works all of them
in all men . . . there are many parts, but one body" (1 Cor. 12:4–
6, 20). The common theme that ties all things together is that
the various ministries and services performed by people filled
with the Spirit of God are Christ-like and to God's glory.

Before writing his short paragraph about being "under the
influence" of God's Spirit instead of intoxicating spirits, Paul had
already referred to the Holy Spirit a number of times in Ephesians.
"You were marked in him with a seal, the promised Holy Spirit,
who is a deposit guaranteeing our inheritance until the
redemption of those who are God's possession—to the praise
of his glory" (1:13b, 14). "For through [Christ] we both have access
to the Father by one Spirit" (2:18). "And in [Christ Jesus] you
too are being built together to become a dwelling in which God
lives by his Spirit" (2:22). "I pray that out of his glorious riches
he may strengthen you with power through his spirit in your
inner being" (3:16). "Make every effort to keep the unity of the
Spirit through the bond of peace" (4:3). "And do not grieve the
Holy Spirit of God, with whom you were sealed for the day of

redemption" (4:30). Then, as an immediate preface to this paragraph: "(for the fruit of the light [light=a likely metaphor for the Spirit of Christ] consists in all goodness, righteousness and truth)" (5:9).

The goodness, righteousness, and truth which the Spirit of God produces in the characters of those who are yielded to his indwelling presence stand in sharp contrast to the debauchery of the sinful nature as stimulated by wine or other things that lead us to be crazy with sin. It is a filling by the Spirit of God that changes our lives to make us more like our Savior, so that we live (5:15, 16) and think (v. 17) and speak (vv. 19, 20) in ways appropriate to the name we are wearing—Christian.

In this chapter we pick up where we left off in the previous one. There we explored the general nature of the Spirit's presence in the children of God. We saw his role in helping us battle the enemy within (that is, the "sinful nature") according to a "new way" God has made possible in Christ. As we set the stage now to explore each of the separate qualities which arise from the indwelling of the Spirit in believers, and how we can cooperate with God in allowing all nine to become realities in our lives, we need to understand what Paul taught in Romans 7 and 8.

Devoted children of a loving Father want to be "under the influence"—not of wine, but of the Spirit. We want to be "under the influence"—not of the sinful nature, but of the sanctified nature in Christ. We long to live "under the influence"—not of the spirit of this world, but of the Spirit of God. We crave to live "under the influence"—not of darkness, but of light.

> The basic problem faced by the child of God is that although the Spirit of God has taken up residence in his life, the old nature has not been removed. Thus a conflict is set up between the old man (what he was when dominated by his sinful nature) and the new man (what he is becoming as he lives under the control of the Spirit). Whenever a Christian allows his sinful nature to control his life in any way he is taking sides with the enemy. Sin is treason. It is forsaking God to serve the enemy (Robert H. Mounce. *Themes From Romans*. Ventura, CA: Regal Books, 1981, p. 88).

Our very bodies are battlegrounds. The old nature still has its remnants in me, but I am indwelt by Someone who is new and holy to God. For me to side with my old sin-ridden nature is going AWOL from God. To side with the new Spirit-led nature is victory. Only the Spirit can make us holy. We cannot do it in our own strength and striving.

The standards for righteousness we sometimes impose on one another usually serve only to hinder the Spirit's work in making us truly righteous. If I am allowed to decide for you that holiness must be so many prayers, so many hours of Bible study, so many contacts for sharing Christ, so many doors knocked, so many good deeds done, so many dollars given—then, to the degree that you attempt to measure up to the standard I create, you are conforming, not to the will of God and the leading of his Spirit, but to me. To the degree that you yield your will to me, you take yourself away from the possibility of letting righteousness occur by being yielded to the presence of the Spirit of God. You would be yielding to the wrong thing. You would be yielding to someone who is just as weak and sinful and prone to error as you are. Only the Spirit of God can make holy, and we cap the well of his overflowing beauty and righteousness when we try to insist that the waters of sanctification must be channeled through our pipes. A teacher is only that—a *teacher.* The real power to create holiness is divine.

The figure of righteousness as an overflowing well of water comes from Jesus himself. "Whoever believes in me," he once said, ". . . streams of living water will flow from within him" (John 7:38). The apostle John commented on his statement: "By this he meant the Spirit, whom those who believed in him were later to receive" (John 7:39a). The presence of the Spirit of God in the lives of his people is comparable to an artesian well bubbling up to eternal life. The power of it is an internal power to each person.

Holiness is not something for us to regiment by our rules of the spiritual road and to enforce as ecclesiastical policemen. We can simply point each other to the statements the Spirit of God has said about righteousness in the Word. We can teach and exhort and hold up as the ideal the personality of Christ as he is revealed there. We can point to characters and incidents where the Spirit of God has put his stamp of approval on certain actions that saints and martyrs of days past have taken that were right and holy. But the ability to produce that same character and those same works in our lives is a power that will have to come from the Spirit of God himself.

This is precisely why the matter of salvation is a personal responsibility between each individual and the Lord. Thus, Paul could exhort: ". . . continue to work out your salvation with fear and trembling" (Phil. 2:12). What? Are we to revert to what the previous chapter in this book called the "old way" of justification by works? Never! For Paul continued in the next verse: "For it is God who works in you to will and to act according to his good purpose" (v. 13). As saved people, we work out our own salvation by giving God the room to work in our lives to bear spiritual fruit, in the season appropriate to our varying levels of maturity and in the way that gives him the greatest glory.

It is much easier if you have a set of negotiated rules and insist that everybody march in lockstep to them. But what you have at the end is not the fruit of the Spirit but the conformity of the flesh. That conformity of the flesh has too long been the goal of too many who have preached the ideal of Christian holiness and sanctification. It is more beautiful and joyous when, as the Lord said, the presence of God's Spirit overflows as water springing up to eternal life.

The Believer's Basic Problem

Paul's personal experience in this matter is related in Romans 7. Here is a brief survey of the problem he saw at work in human experience.

He raises the matter early in the chapter of the life of a God-seeking individual in relation to law. The specific law he has in mind at this point is clearly the law of Moses, because he cites specific commandments out of the Decalogue. He uses a rather typical Pauline literary device of imagining some objector taking issue with what he has already said. Then he replies to the hypothetical objection.

The imagined question, in light of the first six chapters of Romans where justification by faith has been explained, is this: "If righteousness comes by being in Christ and having Christ in us rather than by conformity to a legal standard, then what is your opinion of divine law? Are you saying that law has no place in a Christian's life? Are you downplaying obedience? Are you teaching that conformity to the things God has revealed to be right and holy is not worth stressing? *What shall we say, then? Is the law sin?"*

Paul's answer is direct and nonevasive: "Certainly not!" (7:7a). As to his true sentiment about divine law, it was this: "The law is holy, and the commandment is holy, righteous and good" (v. 12). Neither Paul nor any faithful teacher of the Word of God would ever say disparaging things about what has been revealed in the Ten Commandments or through any other communication from heaven to humanity.

The problem with a believer's inability to be righteous is not that the law is bad, wrong, or inappropriate to its purpose. Every commandment God has ever given us is holy, righteous, and good. The problem is that the people responsible for keeping the law are weak and sinful. "We know that the law is spiritual; but I am unspiritual, sold as a slave to sin" (v. 14). Of course the law is good. Of course obedience is right. The problem is not the *law* but the *law-keeper.* If there is a problem with the law itself, it is that it is too good. Divine law reflects God's own holiness, and we cannot live perfectly holy lives.

Paul develops this theme in Romans at some length and in an intensely personal way.

> So I find this law at work: When I want to do good, evil is right there with me. For in my inner being I delight in God's law; but I see another law at work in the members of my body, waging war against the law of my mind and making me a prisoner of the law of sin at work within my members. What a wretched man I am! (7:21–24a).

Paul had crucified the old man, but that old man wouldn't lie down and die. He had renounced the sinful nature, but the sinful nature would not renounce him. And he never once put the blame on God or God's law. God is perfect, and his laws are perfect. But Paul was wretchedly imperfect. And so is Rubel. And so is Helen. And so is Robert. And so are *you.*

Here, then, is the believer's basic problem: "So then, I myself in my mind am a slave to God's law, but in the sinful nature a slave to the law of sin" (7:25b). In my mind I am committed to the holiness that belongs to God alone and which is revealed in the law which puts his will into words. But the man who tries to keep that law is enslaved to something that is in contradiction to the holiness of God as embodied in that law. He is enslaved to flesh, to the sinful nature, to everything that is in opposition to God.

Discouraging, isn't it? Here is Paul—a saint, an apostle, one of the few people we could look at and say we know he is a holy man—and even *he* admits that he struggles!

Struggle as we must, we need not despair. There is a solution for this seemingly losing conflict between my mind's commitment to the holy laws of God and my flesh's weakness in turning back to the sinful nature. And the cure is not deeper penitence, mortification of the flesh, a longer list of rules, and a daily monitoring system by the people around me. The answer is through the person of Jesus Christ. You can almost hear Paul's shout as he dictates his epistle to a secretary: "Who will rescue me from this body of death? Thanks be to God—through Jesus Christ our Lord!" (7:24b–25a).

God's Rich Provision

How Jesus Christ accomplishes in us what we cannot accomplish for ourselves is related in Romans 8. The story of victory begins on this positive note: "Therefore, there is now no condemnation for those who are in Christ Jesus, because through Christ Jesus the law of the Spirit of life set me free from the law of sin and death" (8:1, 2).

Living the old way was hopeless. Trying to measure up to a perfect law by our weak and sinful strivings could only bring condemnation. That procedure for seeking righteousness— whether under the Decalogue, a patriarchal system, or the gospel of Christ—is nothing more than "the law of sin and death." But in Christ Jesus there is no condemnation, because in Christ Jesus there is a new Spirit working. The key expression is *in Christ Jesus.* Those who are in Christ are not in the stranglehold of sin and death; the Holy Spirit has set them free from that and has given them life. Notice, in fact, that he is called the *"Spirit of life."* The Spirit *is* life, *creates* life, *sustains* life.

The function of the life-giving Spirit relates directly to the work Jesus did in the flesh.

> For what the law was powerless to do in that it was weakened by our sinful nature, God did by sending his own Son in the likeness of sinful man to be a sin offering. And so he condemned sin in sinful man, in order that the righteous requirements of the law might be fully met in us, who do not live according to our sinful nature but according to the Spirit (8:3, 4).

When it was manifestly impossible for us to live up to that perfect standard of righteousness, God took the burden on himself to do it for us. God came in the flesh in the person of Jesus Christ and lived a life that honored divine law perfectly. By doing that, Jesus "condemned sin in sinful man." He joined battle with sin in a body of real flesh, defeated it in personal victory over temptation, and vanquished its power once and for all on the cross by offering himself as a sacrificial lamb (that is, "a sin offering").

Those of us who are in Christ have experienced a swapping of status with Jesus. We gave our sin to him when we accepted him as our Savior and his death on the cross as the atonement for our sin. And in exchange for our sinfulness, he gave us his righteousness. All the righteous requirements of law that we could never meet have been satisfied by him. And that complete righteousness has now been credited to us by virtue of the atonement.

As a result of that finished work of Jesus, Paul says we are left with the following choice of lifestyles:

> Those who live according to their sinful nature have their minds set on what that nature desires; but those who live in accordance with the Spirit have their minds set on what the Spirit desires. The mind of sinful man is death, but the mind controlled by the Spirit is life and peace; the sinful mind is hostile to God. It does not submit to God's law, nor can it do so. Those controlled by the sinful nature cannot please God (8:5-8).

Strong language, isn't it? The person who has been saved by Christ but who, by a conscious choice, decides to keep living the old way, will not be made Christ-like. The one who persists in living a life dominated by the sinful nature, living in rejection of God's law, will not have the changes brought about in him that God is seeking to effect. There will be no fruit of the Spirit in him.

Everybody lives by his or her own choice. There is no escaping it. You live by a choice. I live by a choice. Every day we choose either to live by our sinful nature or to live under the influence of the Spirit of God (v. 5). Choosing to live by the sinful nature is to have what the apostle calls "the mind of sinful man" (v. 6). Such a mind is hostile to God and will not submit to God's law (8:7); indeed, such a mind *cannot* submit to God's law (v. 8). That is not only strong language but frightening language as well.

Anyone who chooses to resist the Spirit by living to satisfy his or her sinful nature cannot bear spiritual fruit, cannot be holy. The inevitable end of making that choice is "death" (v. 6a). If your mind is oriented that way, you simply cannot please God. You cannot walk in the Spirit, you cannot produce fruit, and you cannot be holy. All you can get for your effort is death. On the other hand, the mind which is controlled and transformed by the Spirit experiences not death but "life and peace" (v. 6b).

Frustration is wanting to be holy—and knowing that righteous living is your obligation—but, at the same time, knowing you are not holy and feeling that the harder you try the further away you are from the goal. That is the way things are when you think you have to conform to God's perfect law in your own strength. "The hurrier you go the behinder you get" in your spiritual adventure. Trying to fight a spiritual battle in the strength of flesh keeps you perpetually frustrated and leads to death. Having chosen to live under the influence of the Spirit of God, though, the frustration goes away and your mind comes to be settled and peaceful. The beauty of life by the Spirit of God, like living water springing up within you, begins to be apparent. Both you and everyone touched by your life are refreshed by its overflowing abundance.

The victorious result of life on a new plane by a new principle is this: "You, however, are controlled not by the sinful nature but by the Spirit, if the Spirit of God lives in you" (Rom. 8:9a). Yielded child of God, you have made your choice. You are not going to live by the sinful nature. Neither are you going to try to be holy in the power and strength of a sinful nature anymore.

You are surrendering daily to the Spirit of God to let him live in you. You have your mind focused on that which the Spirit desires. You are learning to rely on his power rather than your own for victory over temptation and fruitfulness to God's glory.

People who live this new way demonstrate that they belong to Christ. People who do not 'have this personal presence and dynamic power in them do not belong to him. "And if anyone does not have the Spirit of Christ, he does not belong to Christ" (8:9b). That statement is as strong a refutation as I know about in Scripture of the notion that somehow the Spirit of God comes to you subsequent to salvation as some form of "second blessing." Contrary to the idea that he comes to you at some later point of maturity and receptivity, the Bible teaches that the Spirit is given to you at the very instant you become a child of God. God sends his Spirit into your heart. At the point of one's repentance and baptism into Christ, the gift of the Holy Spirit is given then and there (Acts 2:38). "Because you are sons, God sent the Spirit of his Son into our hearts, the Spirit who calls out, 'Abba, Father'" (Gal. 4:6).

The practical difference in the life of someone indwelt by the living presence of the Holy Spirit is all-important. In a word, the difference in the non-indwelt person and the Spirit-filled one is *life*.

> But if Christ is in you, your body is dead because of sin, yet your spirit is alive because of righteousness. And if the Spirit of him who raised Jesus from the dead is living in you, he who raised Christ from the dead will also give life to your mortal bodies through his Spirit, who lives in you (Rom. 8:10, 11).

Do you believe God has great power? Of course you do. Why? The one fact above all others which testifies to divine power is the resurrection. The world took Jesus, nailed him to a cross, took his life away, and sealed him in a tomb. It appeared that dismal Friday to be all over. Saturday came and passed, and he was still entombed, as his enemies reflected on their finest hour. But God's power was greater than Satan's, greater than sin, greater than the Romans, greater than the high priests of the Jews. So on Sunday morning God raised him up by a mighty display of his power. Already in the Roman epistle, Paul had identified himself as a servant of the one "who through the Spirit of holiness was declared with power to be the Son of God by his resurrection from the dead: Jesus Christ our Lord" (1:4).

In Paul's mind there was no way of separating the presence of the Holy Spirit from the display of divine power. If God's power had been displayed, as in the resurrection, it was because the Spirit of God was present. Wherever the Spirit of God is present, power will be in evidence. Think, then, about our situation. The same Holy Spirit who raised Christ Jesus from the dead is living in us to give power, might, and life to our mortal bodies (8:11).

The same power that raised Jesus from the dead is present to give you victory over the desires of the flesh right now, to give you the ability to break loose from the shackles of addiction, to enable you to walk away from relationships that are unholy and which must be broken. In the weakness of your mortal body and its willpower, determination, and resolve, you haven't been able to cope with those. In the power of God's Spirit, you can.

The same power that raised Jesus from the dead is present to transform your personality from depressed to vibrant, to enable you to do good works that glorify God, to empower you as his instrument to lead lost souls to the Lamb of God who takes away the sin of the world. As surely as you believe God has power, you can believe that he has harnessed that power for your sake.

You are God's child. The Spirit of God is in you. You have chosen to walk under his influence, rather than under the control of your sinful nature. The same power that raised Jesus from the dead is active in you. Therefore, you must see your life in an entirely new perspective. Paul begins: "Therefore, brothers, we have an obligation" (8:12a).

Hold on, Paul. Wait just a minute! Didn't you denounce obligation back in chapter 7? Didn't you say we wouldn't be saved by our obedience and good works? Didn't you say the work of salvation was entirely of grace and received by faith alone?

What Paul denounced in Romans 7 was the widely held (both then and now) scheme of redemption which predicates salvation on human merit within a system of works-righteousness. He did not denounce the idea of obligation. Everybody has an obligation to something. Even the Spirit-led person, who has been set free from condemnation by virtue of being in Christ, has an obligation. He or she must simply be clear about the nature of the obligation. There is no such thing as independent, self-motivating, self-directing man. Everybody gives himself away to something else to conform to it, live under its influence, and be obligated to it.

> Before salvation, man was controlled by his sinful nature. After salvation, control was turned over to the Spirit of God. At no time has man been absolutely free to do whatever he wants. He acts in conformity to what he was (fallen and therefore sinful) or to what he has become in Christ (a new man fashioned in righteousness). Autonomous man is a myth. There exists no state of moral neutrality which allows freedom of choice apart from the pressures of sin or the Spirit. . . . One might paraphrase the challenge of Elijah, "Choose you this day which life-controlling force you will obey: your sinful nature which leads to death or the indwelling spirit who leads to life" (see 1 Kings 18:21). (Mounce. *Themes from Romans.* p. 90.)

The "obligation" of a blood-purchased and Spirit-filled person is clear. We owe nothing more to the old nature and everything to God. Our obligation is to carry out the wishes of the Spirit in whose power and under whose control we live.

> Therefore, brothers, we have an obligation—but it is not to the sinful nature, to live according to it. For if you live according to the sinful nature, you will die; but if by the Spirit you put to death the misdeeds of the body, you will live, because those who are led by the Spirit of God are sons of God. For you did not receive a spirit that makes you a slave again to fear, but you received the Spirit of sonship. And by him we cry, "Abba, Father." The Spirit himself testifies with our spirit that we are God's children. Now if we are children, then we are heirs—heirs of God and co-heirs with Christ, if indeed we share in his sufferings in order that we may also share in his glory (8:12–17).

The presence and activity of the Spirit of God in us proves that we are God's sons. From this, Paul takes the next logical step: If we are his sons, then we are his heirs. Heirs! Not slaves trying to earn status, but sons who are heirs by virtue of family connection. We have status because of who we are, not what we have done. Praise God! There is no more beautiful or liberating truth in all his Holy Word.

The Spirit: God's Answer to Inward Flaws

We human beings really have two problems—the fact that we have sinned and the fact that we are sinners. Sometimes we only want to deal with one of the problems and ignore the other. The fact that we have sinned is dealt with when we accept Christ. But how do we deal with the deeper problem that we are sinful in our disposition, our habits, our lifestyle? That is what the biblical "gift of the Holy Spirit" is about.

The Spirit of God is given to deal with the deeper, larger problem. The blood of Jesus Christ forgives the past. The presence of the Spirit of God takes away fear when you start looking at the future. In the place of our fear, he instills confidence— testifying with our spirits that we are God's children. And because we are his children, we are his heirs and can live victoriously.

Christians often fail today to change the inner man because they use methods of law which Paul said were inadequate. . . . They list for themselves a few commandments or rules of conduct and they obey them rigidly each week (sing, pray, give, commune, attend, etc.). *But they remain the same inwardly year after year.* Like the Pharisee, who fasted, gave tithes, and prayed each week, they are not changed in the inner man. Their covenant is a covenant of law. It is not a personal allegiance to the Master and they are not walking after the Spirit. Their covenant is ineffective in two respects: They get very little done in the way of outward obedience, and very little improvement in the inner man. *They may be just as covetous, hateful, and lustful as they ever were.*

Thus, a personal indwelling of the Spirit, as a provision for the inner man's needs, becomes a necessary belief in working out our salvation; in establishing a covenant with Christ; in crucifying the old man; in growing the fruit of the Spirit (Bert Mercer. "The Indwelling Spirit," *Image.* July 1, 1985. p. 9).

God has dealt effectively with both our needs. He has cleansed and justified us. He has given his Spirit to work from within us to gradually transform us and make us more like his incomparable Son, Jesus. To live "under the influence" of the divine Spirit of holiness is to experience life, peace, and joy.

Conclusion

Perhaps an analogy will help pull all this together. If you have had children who have passed through their teenage years, you can understand and plug into it. If you are not that old, perhaps you can remember back to your own teen years.

Imagine a typical child who has to be told every move to make. He has to be told to wash his face, scrub behind his ears, use some shampoo on his hair, brush his teeth, brush his hair. You pretty well have to monitor every move. It seems hopeless at times and appears that he will never grow up. Sometimes you think about an experiment to see just how long he would live in his own filth before he would bathe and pick up his room. (The experiment always fails because conditions get beyond the parents' point of tolerance long before the child's.) Every step has to be dictated by the parents, and it is only against the child's will that the shower door is opened, the soap is scrubbed on, and the shampoo is used.

But glorious marvel of marvels! Wonder of wonders! One day he starts bouncing out of bed and going into the shower as his first order of business. He doesn't just shampoo but conditions his hair as well. He doesn't just brush his hair but parts and sprays it. He doesn't just brush his teeth but rinses with mouthwash. He has fallen in love. And the things that a watchful, observant, well-intentioned parent once had to drive the child to do are now done without the need of a reminder or threat. They flow as naturally from the changed heart of that person, the changed focus of that boy's attention, as anything could.

That is Romans 7 and 8 in a nutshell. Paul confessed that he once tried to bring himself and others to holiness before God by pointing to the rules and threatening. He resisted the process and saw that everybody else did, too. Then he learned that there could be a different perspective on the whole matter of righteousness. He discovered that something could happen in the heart of a person which would make him do by a new nature the very things that his old nature had resisted.

What happens is this: The love of Christ opens one's heart and God fills that open heart with his indwelling Spirit. With the Spirit of God functioning as a new dynamic within his being, that person comes to do by his new nature what his old nature did only partially—and then, kicking and screaming.

Can you testify to the same achievement in your life? If you have gone through the process, you understand how it happens. And now you know how wonderful it is to live "under the influence" of God's Spirit and to see the fruit of his presence in your daily experience.

3
Love

When some people talk about the Holy Spirit and his presence in the life of a Christian, the first question they ask is: "How *high* did he make you *jump*?" That's the wrong question. The correct query is: "How *straight* is he making you *walk*?"

The purpose for the Spirit's presence in the heart and life of a believer is to produce Christ-like character. He is not among us to make us do bizarre and supernatural things, but to enable us to exhibit divine beauty in the characters we form, the relationships we live in, and the churches we build.

As opposed to the "acts of the sinful nature," which characterize people living to satisfy their own lusts, Paul identifies the "fruit of the Spirit," which will be borne in the lives of people living to the glory of God. It is significant that Paul uses the singular word *fruit* rather than the expected plural form. This likely means that these qualities are a unity. Like grapes, rather than separate pieces of fruit, they come in a cluster. Unlike the miraculous "gifts" of the Spirit which were given one by one according to the need of the earliest church, these traits are all found in all of God's children.

Just as we might have expected, *love* is the first item in the list of these nine qualities. It is the one that binds everything else together in perfect unity.

The Godlike Virtue

The Bible affirms that God *is* love (1 John 4:8). That affirmation is not intended to deny personality to God and present our deity as an abstraction. God is personal. If, however, you were to choose a single word to define the essence of his character, that word would have to be **love**.

If you were asked to choose one word to describe the characters of *some* people you know, you might come up with words like *aggressive, shy, bright, obnoxious,* or *greedy.* If you were to choose one word to describe God, the most appropriate one you could ever find would be this one: love.

And God wants people who know him to participate in his nature. "Hear, O Israel: The LORD our God, the LORD is one. Love the LORD your God with all your heart and with all your soul and with all your strength" (Deut. 4, 5).

When an expert in the law of Moses asked him about "the greatest commandment in the law," Jesus quoted the *shema* from Deuteronomy 6. He identified the obligation to love God with one's whole being as the "first and greatest commandment." He then identified the second commandment for the man: "Love your neighbor as yourself." In this case, he was quoting Leviticus 19:18. He concluded "All the Law and the Prophets hang on these two commandments" (Matt. 22:37–40).

The two commandments on which everything hangs can be reduced to one word: *love.* Love your God and love your neighbor, and you become a medium for the presence of God in the world.

The priority of love among Christian virtues lay behind Paul's affirmation: "And now these three remain: faith, hope and love. But the greatest of these is love" (1 Cor. 13:13). Remembering that there were no chapter divisions when Paul originally wrote his epistles, the next line immediately exhorts us: "Follow the way of love" (14:1a).

Since love is the greatest thing, since it is the very essence of God's perfect nature, since God's desire is to make us channels of his love—follow after it, pursue it, seek it, desire it, develop it, and nurture it.

Condemned by the Law of Love

All of us stand condemned by the law of love, for not one of us loves as he or she ought to love. Perhaps you are ready to reply, "Speak for yourself, Rubel." I do! Of all the commands that God has ever given, there is not one before which I feel quite so inadequate as this one.

Ironic, isn't it? The law of love—which is the law that allows God to accept me—is the same law that puts me under the greatest condemnation. I love God, but my behavior proves that I do not always love him with all my being. I love my neighbor, too, but sometimes I fail to love him as much as I love myself and wind up protecting my interests against his needs.

Paul spoke of certain laws that he admitted were spiritual and holy but which, nevertheless, caused him problems. He chose "You shall not covet" as a case in point of a law he acknowledged to be good but admitted to violating at times.

Let's take another commandment and analyze it from our experience: "Love God with your whole being." I reflect on it, and I know there could be no greater commandment. I know it is right. It is holy. It is spiritual. But who among us does not stand under condemnation before this just command because of our inability to do better?

Now think about your relationship to the second commandment: "Love your neighbor as you love yourself." You stand condemned by it. You don't always love people the same way you love yourself. All of us are far more critical of our neighbors than of ourselves. We tend to be much quicker to believe the worst of others, while putting the best possible interpretation on the things we say or do. We tend to be slower to forgive them than to forgive ourselves.

> To be condemned by love is a terrible irony, for love is the very power of acceptance. But we are condemned by love when it comes to us only in the form of a law, because it is the most utterly impossible of all laws. None of us can make it as persons who care for others with utter disregard for any reward for ourselves. The only way to cope with love as a law is to experience it first as a gift. (Lewis B. Smedes. *Love Within Limits*. Grand Rapids: William B. Eerdmans Publishing Co., 1978, p. 149).

Love must *enable* us before it can *obligate* us. What some of us have missed—even though we are new covenant people who are of the Spirit rather than the letter—is that we too often struggle with a number of commandments at the level of law

without first confronting them in the person of Jesus and as
a gift that we both receive and bestow.

Natural Love

Most of the love in our lives is need-love. It arises from a
need in the lover. It reaches to someone or something that
promises to fill a need within our experiences.

Take the love of friends as an example. I need friends. There
are social impulses within me that go begging without friendships
in my life. So I am willing to be nice and do favors for John
because I need something from him. I need him to give those
back to me in kind. *I* need some favors occasionally. I need
acceptance. I need to be able to talk my heart out to somebody.
John needs the same kindnesses, so we establish a give-and-take
relationship. It is need-love in both of us that causes us to go
seeking friendships and to develop them. All of us experience
this phenomenon and can understand it from personal history.

The type of love all of us experience most of the time in
the purest of our relationships is need-love. It gives in the
expectation that the loved one or the loved thing will give back.

Even the dearest and noblest love we experience at a natural
level is rooted in need. My wife and I chose to have children,
and we love them with genuine devotion. But our decision to
have children was not a totally unselfish thing. It was not our
exclusive motivation to bring three children into the world so
we could give to them, do for them, and extend ourselves for
their sakes. That was certainly part of our understanding of what
having children would mean—but it was not the only thing in
our minds. We wanted a need filled in us that we believed could
only be satisfied if we had children both to love and by whom
to be loved.

Surely the love we feel for God has personal need at its heart.
Lost sinners do not love God altruistically and unselfishly. We
love God because we feel a need for him. Reaching out to him
and extending ourselves for him, we are confident he is able
to reach back. We are sure that he is going to give more than
we are offering up.

This sort of love is not evil. It is natural. It is the common
and dominant way all of us love in all of our relationships. We
have certain voids that can be filled by love alone, and we are

intelligent enough to know we can get love only if we give love. This level of love is right and holy, for it moves us out of our confining egos to seek, communicate, and give.

Jesus exhibited need-love. Why do you think he formed friendships? Why do you think he went to Bethany to be with Mary, Martha, and Lazarus so frequently, rather than just spending the night wherever he was? They were special friends. And he both gave and received love when he was with them. Their home must have been something of a retreat for him. It must have been a comfortable, warm place he could go in his turbulent life. He had friends, and they met needs in his life.

Why do you think he chose the Twelve? It was because of a need-love within him. He sought men who could be both helpers and friends in the great work he had come to do.

The Father from heaven admitted to need-love in relation to the Son of Man. In connection with his baptism at the hands of John the Baptizer, he said, "You are my Son, whom I love; with you I am well-pleased" (Mark 1:11). That is the sort of love I feel for my children when they do something that pleases me. I am not initiating love but receiving it. Thus in response I say, "I like that. I appreciate you. You are my beloved son. You are my special daughter. Well done!" There is nothing unholy about love at that level.

The danger with need-love is that it can be bent and perverted so easily. Need-love, if we don't watch it and monitor it closely, can lead us into using people. Because we need certain favors, we can bait and be generous with people so as to manipulate them to our ends. And that is evil. It is not wrong to have needs that others can fill in your life, but it is wrong to have those needs filled by exploiting people. Greed and lust are very obvious examples of how need-love can go wrong and be perverted.

There is another way to love, however, which is higher, purer, and more spiritual than need-love. And if need-love is love in its *natural* form, then surely it is not improper to call this higher form *super*-natural love.

Supernatural Love

The sort of love described to this point could be represented in the language in which the New Testament was written by two or three different words. One of them is *erōs*. Although it is the term from which we get English words like "erotic," it is not a sinister word at all. *Erōs* is simply desire toward some person or thing. That desire does not have to be wicked. Another is *philia*, friendship love. And still a third is *storgē*, a word referring to the sort of natural affection we feel for those closest to us. The natural love spoken of to this point could be described with any one of these words.

But Christianity picked up a word that was rarely used in the Greek vocabulary of New Testament days and elevated that word to a status that makes it unique in Christian vocabulary. The highest and divine form of love is what the New Testament calls *agapē*.

Agapē is selfless love. It arises—not from a need within self, but from a need in the other. One sees a need someone else has and willingly expends himself to satisfy it. One who loves on the level of *agapē* does so expecting nothing in return. It seeks no reward. The give-and-take love that is common on the natural level gives way to the give-and-get-nothing love on a supernatural level.

Love at the natural level always expects something in return. One will blatantly tell his friend, "Now, wait a minute. I did so-and-so for you, and I think I have a right to expect you to do this for me." Parents tell their children, "After all I've done for you, are you going to turn around and talk to me that way? How dare you! After all I've done for you!" At the common level of love, we all expect something back from the love we give.

Agapē, on the other hand, gives and expects no reward. It does not give for the sake of getting. It does not invest in hope of a dividend. It just *gives*.

The perfect model of supernatural love is Jesus Christ. He loved freely. He loved unselfishly. He loved for the sake of those who needed love. How could his love have been motivated by selfishness? What need did Jesus have that could have been satisfied by what he did? Could he achieve higher status in all the universe than the status he had before coming to earth? Were there needs in his personality that were empty until he came and rubbed shoulders with humanity?

Jesus saw needs we had and could not satisfy. Expecting no rewards, making no demands, setting no preconditions—he came to save us out of self-emptying love.

I stand condemned under the obligation to love as Jesus loved. Now, I can love at a friendship level. I can give love so long as I am getting it back, and friendship will grow stronger through reciprocity in the relationship. I can love within my family. I can love within the church. In all these situations, I am having needs met by giving love—and getting love back in return.

It isn't that I never love unselfishly and without expecting something in return, mind you, but I can't love that way all the time. Unless there is some getting as well as giving, I burn out. My resources become depleted.

Only a love as pure as God's is powerful enough to inspire in human beings the desire to exhibit selfless love. When I see the kind of love Jesus lived so constantly, the desire is generated in me to love more on that model and less on the purely natural level. I really mean it when I tell myself that I want to replace need-love with more of the love which is selfless, self-emptying, and free of conditions. But sometimes I just get tired and say, "I've given all I can give today." Sometimes I take the phone off the hook. Have you ever felt that way? Can you understand at all what I am describing?

God loves us when we cannot love him back, when we can't love each other, or when we just can't do loving things that we know we ought to be doing. It isn't that we don't want to love after his example. It is just that we sometimes can't do it. When we are at our best as loving creatures, there are only so many hours in a day and only so many places we can get to within those hours.

As long as we live on planet Earth, it will be this way. The only time we will ever to able to love fully is when we are in a different sphere of existence than we can experience now; when we are closer to God than we can be now; when we don't have the limitations we have to accept now.

So long as we live in the flesh, it is only by the power of the Holy Spirit in us that we can move from need-love to *agapē* love. Seeing that sort of love in Jesus inspires us in the direction of selfless love, but it takes divine power to empower that sort of love in us. That is why love is a fruit of the Spirit.

Living in Love

Although we are commanded to love, although we see love

in God, and although we want to love in this divine manner—
we cannot love purely until we have the Spirit of God in us
to enable and empower us. Christians can live in love because
we have a power in us which is greater than the power of the
flesh and our sinful nature.

Sometimes it may be true that even Christians help people
and preach the gospel only out of some form of need-love in
us that expects something back. We attach strings. We demand
to see results. So sometimes we bring missionaries home who
are working in a difficult place because we aren't seeing enough
conversions. Sometimes we do benevolent work with the
condition that the persons receiving help attend our assemblies
or become members of the congregation. Yes, it is possible to
do spiritual things at the level of our sinful, carnal nature.

The kind of love God exhibits (and the sort we are supposed
to be moving toward) is love which says, "If I have something
to give, I refuse to give it with strings attached. This is not
being done for the sake of baiting a hook to put into your mouth."

Love is the guideline for the liberties we have in Christ, too.
Because of Christ, I am free. I have liberties. I have privileges.
But selfless love will cause me to forego some of those rights.

Paul talked about his "liberties" as a Christian both in Romans
and First Corinthians. Summing up what he said on the topic,
he said that believers should avoid passing judgment on one
another in disputed topics (Rom. 14:1-4) and emphasized that
stronger Christians have a special duty to weaker and immature
believers (vv. 5-18; 1 Cor. 8:1-13). Furthermore, some beliefs are
best kept between the individual and his Lord if airing them
is likely to stir discord and strife (Rom. 14:19-23; 1 Cor. 10:23-
24). The guiding principle about the use of a liberty in Christ
must be love for the brethren (Rom. 15:1, 2; 1 Cor. 10:31-11:1).

Perhaps the key verse in all Paul said on the topic is this
one: "Knowledge puffs up, but love builds up" (1 Cor. 8:1b). This
verse is pivotal because it contrasts our normal tendency with
our spiritual obligation. The normal tendency of human beings
is to weigh options, decide on a personal course of action, and
move forward. Thus, in some disputable area of Christian
behavior, I form a conviction based on my study.

For the sake of illustration, let the issue at hand be the moderate
use of alcoholic beverages. I *know* that table wines are not
intrinsically evil and that Jesus of Nazareth drank such beverages

on occasion. My "knowledge" may puff me up, push me ahead, and draw some weak brother to his spiritual destruction. Even if I could drink in moderation and never become drunk or do anything to harm another person directly, my influence might well cause a brother who has a real problem with alcohol to use it to his damnation. A loving person who is being led by the Spirit may choose to forego his right for the sake of others who might be harmed—even if only indirectly—by his deed.

Love is also the ground for unity in the body of Christ. We seem to labor under the general misperception that the basis for unity in Christ is having everybody think alike, act alike, and be alike—with "alikeness" measured by the beliefs and behaviors of the speaker or writer. And that is precisely why the church of the Lord Jesus is fragmented. There will never be unity based on conformity, for we simply are not alike, do not think alike, and cannot be alike.

The goal of spiritual maturity in Christ is personal likeness to him. When we get to the point that we can substitute similarity to one another for likeness to him, we will have erred from the faith.

Truth is all-important to the Christian faith, for it is through propositional truth (that is, Scripture) that we approach personal truth (Jesus). But since our ability to discover, grasp, and practice propositional truth varies in light of countless variables, we will never all stand at the same spot on the road which leads to him who is truth personified. Some will be far in front, and many of us will trail behind; some will stand squarely in the center of the path, and others of us will occasionally wander to one side or pursue some fascinating (but distracting) side road; still others will slip and stagger backwards on steep parts of the road. Love rather than lockstep will have to hold us together as we travel.

We are no more the same in the family of God than in the Shelly, Jones, or Baker families. We will have to see ourselves as a family and act as a family on the basis of love.

Love, in fact, is the ideal covering garment worn by the followers of Jesus at all times.

> Therefore, as God's chosen people, holy and dearly loved, clothe yourselves with compassion, kindness, humility, gentleness and patience. Bear with each other and forgive whatever grievances

you may have against one another. Forgive as the Lord forgave
you. And over all these virtues, put on love, which binds them
all together in perfect unity (Col. 3:12–14).

With the flesh (that is, carnal man, sinful nature) crucified
and the new man (Christ-centered, Spirit-filled) center stage, the
old wardrobe appropriate to the former must be discarded in
favor of attire appropriate to the latter. Sexual immorality, lust,
and greed must be put off; anger, slander, and lies must be shed
(see vv. 5–11). In their place may be worn the beautiful articles
of compassion, forgiveness, and the like. And the one distinctive
article which tops off and coordinates all these pieces is love.

I am no expert on fashion. I do know enough, however, to
recognize that one can sometimes lay out articles of clothing
that just don't seem to go together. Their colors clash, and the
eye is almost jarred from its socket by their juxtaposition. Into
that combination of items, however, a fashion expert can bring
one other that picks up a little hint of the color and style of
those discordant parts and creates a stunning outfit. Gorgeous!
Magnificent! That is what love is to Christian personality and
to the body of Christ as a whole.

Here are two individuals—perhaps married to each other,
perhaps in the same church—with contrasting temperaments. No
one in his right mind would ever size them up as likely marriage
partners, co-laborers in the kingdom, or friends. One is brash,
and the other is shy; one is extroverted, and the other is introverted;
one is a ball of fire, and the other is laid back and mellow; one
is wealthy, and the other barely gets by. But they are Christians.
And something incredible is obvious in their relationship.

By the grace of God, their natural dispositions and circumstances have been subordinated to supernatural possibilities. Their
sinful natures are being struggled against by the power of the
indwelling Spirit. In various situations, the naturally aggressive
one has demonstrated unexpected humility, and the natural
introvert has exhibited marvelous boldness to act upon principle.
Each has learned to be patient with the other, and failure is always
healed with unselfish forgiveness. Love is triumphant!

Here is a church filled with different—sometimes conflicting—
people, personalities, interests, and goals. Occasionally it seems
inevitable that elders and deacons are coming to loggerheads,

that the missions committee and the treasurer will have blows. But when that church is a temple for the Spirit of God, gentleness guides through treacherous waters and kindness prevails. No backlog of grievances is allowed to accumulate. The work of God goes on without bickering, suspicion, and division because love is the mantle draped over the entire body!

Deeds Speak Louder Than Words

Agapē love is one's willingness to give of himself for the sake of another's joy, well-being, or growth.

It is easy to see how this definition fits the way God has loved us. Sometimes it is difficult for us to understand how it explains anything at all about our obligation to love one another. Thus, we speak of love as a mystical, undefinable, unknowable something. We engage in a great deal of self-deception about the loving feelings we have for people toward whom we are exhibiting unloving deeds.

It helps tremendously in dealing with this problem to realize that love is not a feeling, but a way of thinking and acting. It is certainly easier and more pleasant to think and act positively toward people for whom you feel affection. The hallmark of Christian *agapē*, however, is its ability to function in the absence of affection. If your love is modeled after God's and empowered by the Holy Spirit, you can take loving and constructive action toward someone you dislike and find repugnant.

Think for a moment of the description of love in 1 Corinthians 13. It does not describe how one feels who acts lovingly, but how one thinks and acts. It communicates the message that love is as love does.

Love is patient and kind. It protects its object. It trusts, hopes, and perseveres. On the negative side, it refuses to be boastful, proud, or envious toward the one who is loved. It will not behave rudely. It will not be selfish and short-tempered. No matter how the person *feels* at the moment, his Spirit-guided love will enable him to persevere in *thinking* and *behaving* so as to do what will bring joy, well-being, and growth to the person he loves.

If you are married and living in love, you understand this principle. Sometimes you don't feel like attending to your mate's needs. You may be tired and hurting. You may not feel like talking through some problem, helping with some chore, or even responding to sexual advances. But, on some occasions at least, you move outside and beyond your feelings to exhibit the loving behavior of patient concern, unselfish assistance, and nurturing acts.

If you are a member of a church which lives in love, you understand this principle, too. Some member may be guilty of a sin which embarrasses the whole body. The action may even have been criminal and splashed on the front page of the newspaper. Yet, knowing that the church is a fraternity of sinners, the actions of the church are loving rather than unloving. Although the feelings of people may tend to cause them to withdraw and protect themselves from being associated with the individual in question, they treat him gently, seek his restoration to the body as a penitent member, and help him put his life back together.

How pitiful to see a man weeping in a bar about how much he loves his family—a family pining away at home for his presence and loving actions. How incongruous to hear Christians speak of how their love for John Doe forces them to behave so unlovingly toward him—actions which grow out of *their* feelings of pain or fear rather than *his* needs. How sickening to read the epithets hurled at brethren in the name of loving the truth— truth whose first obligation on those who are really devoted to it is love.

One whose love for God is a conscious, Spirit-enhanced choice can pray and worship, while the person whose love is conceived as feeling cannot. One whose love for his fellows is a volitional act can return good for evil to an enemy, while the person whose love is emotional will seek revenge.

People who live on the plane of love are not living according to the flesh, but to the Spirit. They have learned the spiritual truth that deeds speak louder than words. They know that love is not a feeling, but a positive pattern of Spirit-led action.

Conclusion

Love is hardly the mushy sentimentality some people have thought—"sloppy *agapē*," someone called it. Love is tough and durable. Love is powerful and creative. Love is the very essence of God.

The only way we will come to have this attitude and behavior in our lives is by the presence of God's Holy Spirit. Since love is the fruit of the Spirit, we will be loving people only as his enabling power is allowed to work in us. We must stop resisting and grieving his attempts to create love among us and pray instead for his work to be realized.

Go ahead and admit that the love which dominates your life is need-love. You tend to give love because you need to get it back. You make investments of love in the lives of other people because you want dividends returned. That's okay! It is the natural thing to do.

Realize however, that there is also a *super*natural love which is generated by the Spirit of God in believers' lives. It is the purest and most divine form of love. It is godlike in nature. With the presence and power of the Holy Spirit in you, you can accept God's unconditional love and begin to let it flow through you to others. Increasingly, there will be times when it dawns on you that you did something that had absolutely no ulterior motive to it or hidden agenda behind it. You weren't expecting anything back. You gave to somebody who will never be able to give anything back. You did something that was qualitatively like what God is always doing for you.

Remember that this new way of loving is *un*natural due to the fact that it is *super*natural. So don't get discouraged with the difficulty of it. Give the Spirit of God time to acclimate you to it. Don't be like some of us have been with jogging. Deciding that we needed to change our state of physical well-being, we put on jogging shoes and hit the streets in a sprint. A few blocks away, with muscles cramping and stomachs aching, we hitchhike home and gasp, "I'll never do that again. It's just impossible for me."

Some of us try to love that way. Learning about the unique nature of Christian *agape* as selfless concern and convicted of our need to improve our spiritual well-being, we commit to self-sacrifice and the 100 percent emptying of ourselves for the sake of God and people around us. Down the road a short distance, we are gasping, cramping, and in pain. We say, "I'll never do that again. It's just impossible for me."

Running and loving are alike in that your output must be matched by your intake.

Running requires oxygen, and an unfit body will use up more oxygen than it can take in by starting a jogging regimen equal to that of a marathon runner. So you start very slowly. You walk more than you run at first. Your initial goal is just to keep moving. As your stamina and strength increase, you begin to cover greater distances without the pain.

Loving requires spiritual intake, and an untrained or immature Christian will use up all his meager resources by trying to start out at the level of the most mature saint he knows. You start very slowly. You walk more than you run at first. Your initial goal is just to keep moving. As you draw increasing strength from the Word of God, the fellowship of the saints, and the presence of the Spirit, you build up your capacity to love after the example of God. Pretty soon the huffing and puffing from short distances will give way to stamina and strength. You will be running marathons. You will be loving as Jesus loved.

As the experiences of godlike love multiply in your life, you will realize that the indwelling Spirit is bearing fruit in you. And you will give God the glory.

The fruit of the Spirit is *love.*

4
Joy

I don't think we emphasize the place of *joy* and rejoicing in Christian experience the way God does in his Word. That is unfortunate. It places those of us who are modern-day teachers of the Scripture under rebuke for slighting an important biblical theme. And it deprives those who listen to us of an impetus to spirituality and holiness that would be invaluable in their sometimes-depressed hearts.

All of us want to be happy. We Americans live in a country whose Declaration of Independence proclaims that our Creator has endowed all human beings with "certain unalienable rights," one of which is "the pursuit of happiness." Survey any age group or socioeconomic level in any part of our country and you will find the same priority item on every list: personal happiness, contentment, gladness, *joy*.

It is not sinful for you to harbor such an ambition, so stop feeling guilty about it. Yes, there are hungry children in India and starving adults on the African continent. There are cancer and burn victims in the local veterans hospital. People live under political repression in many places, and there are Christians in prison for the sake of their public confession of Jesus. By what right, then, can you and I be excused for thinking about the pursuit of joy?

Believe it or not, the cosmos does not revolve around you—
or me. Thus, neither of us has the responsibility of taking all
the hurt of the world to himself. Only God could possibly
undertake such a task. Since he is on the job, we can rest a
bit easier. Rather than brood and exude spiritual melancholy,
we can rejoice that he has taken the sins and sorrows of the
race unto himself—and stand ready to help him in occasional
burden-bearing episodes.

As a matter of fact, we will be more useful to God in helping
others and lifting their burdens if we cultivate joy as a character
trait. Whom do you seek when you need encouragement? The
person who looks doleful and beaten down with life or the one
whose spirit soars above the gloom?

Does Your God Smile?

God wants us to be happy, so it can hardly be inappropriate
for us to desire the same thing. The yearning for gladness in
our lives doesn't have to be a selfish and wicked thing. Jesus
began his Sermon on the Mount with the Beatitudes. And how
many times have you been told that the word *blessed* in our
standard translations would better be translated *happy*? Happy
is the person who can restrain his ego; happy is the man who
is sensitive enough to be able to mourn at appropriate times;
happy is the woman whose spirit is under the gentle restraint
of God, and so forth. If the Lord instructed us in a lifestyle designed
to produce happiness, can it be wrong for us to live that way
and experience the joy which comes of the Spirit's presence in
our hearts?

Try a thought experiment with me for a moment. Close your
eyes briefly, and visualize the face of God. If you say that trying
to visualize the face of a spirit being is impossible for you, let
it be the face of Jesus—God with flesh and bones. Stop reading
right now, lift your eyes from the page, and create that face
in your mind.

What did you see? Was it the face of God as represented by
Michelangelo on the ceiling of the Sistine Chapel? Was it tied
to some artistic representation of Jesus from a picture you saw
as a child? Did you create an original one? Let me ask you to
think back to that face again and focus on the mouth. Is it smiling?

Frankly, I have always tended to visualize him as rather somber and stern-faced. I am trying to learn to visualize him with a gentle, smiling face. And I dare say neither of us typically thinks of God as having his mouth open in laughter.

Yet Paul wrote to Timothy concerning the "glorious gospel of the blessed God, which he entrusted to me" (1 Tim. 1:11). The adjective *blessed* is from the same root word as is used in the Beatitudes. Here, just as in Matthew 5, its fundamental meaning has to do with happiness. So Paul is acknowledging the possession of the gospel (good news) which had been given him by a *happy God.* All of us might be wise to adjust the focus of the mental picture we have of God to get some of that sternness and steeliness off his face to visualize more of the happy radiance which belongs there.

Three years ago I was involved in a project that spent several thousand dollars trying to create a face for Jesus that would be used in hundreds of thousands of pieces of teaching literature. Several early tries from the artist had to be rejected precisely because the face was too stern and forbidding. The acid test of each try was to show the face to children, without telling them who the person was supposed to be, and ask them to tell me what kind of man this was. The early ones got answers like "mad," "mean," or even "ugly." I kept pushing until we came up with a face that had a pleasant mouth and warm eyes. Children finally began using words like "nice" or "friendly"; my favorite response of all was of a little girl who said nothing when she was shown the face but smiled back at it, and walked over and kissed it. Then I knew we had found the right one!

Maybe we would all feel differently about God if we softened his face a bit with the traces of warmth and joy we find so inviting in the faces of people we meet day by day. We serve a happy God, a God who created us with the desire to be happy, a God who has given good news designed to make us happy.

You can't make yourself be happy, can you? You've tried sometimes. You've read the Dale Carnegie books and the Norman Vincent Peale books. They tell you to smile, no matter what. Be happy. Look life in the face every morning and like what you see. You've read the self-help books that give six steps to happiness. And you've taken the six steps—and still felt miserable. You cannot make yourself be happy in life circumstances that are awful. You just can't lift yourself by your bootstraps and be filled with joy when your body is racked with pain. The only way you can experience joy in the really difficult moments of life is for God to generate it within you by the presence of his Spirit. It will not be captured or created by the powers of flesh.

Since joy and happiness are intrinsic to God's nature, the development of these qualities in our lives can be achieved only in relation to him. That is why joy is a fruit of the Spirit of God.

A Virtue Larger than Circumstances

Something that is important, from the beginning, is that we not confuse the joy and happiness the Bible talks about with what *we* generally conceive to be happiness.

In English, the word *happiness* is directly related to the word *happening*. Thus, we can feel happy only if things of a certain positive nature are coming to us in steady succession. If you get a promotion, you're happy. If you buy a new wardrobe, you're happy. If your child is born healthy and beautiful, you're happy. But if you are sick, get passed over for the promotion, lose your job, or have a child born with club feet, you are *not* happy.

As we define and experience happiness in terms of happenings, it must arise from the outside circumstances of life. If things are going well, I can be happy; if things have turned sour, I am miserably unhappy.

In what must have been one of his many moments of melancholy, Solomon reflected on this tendency to link one's spiritual state with human experience. He wrote: "Even in laughter the heart may ache, and joy may end in grief" (Prov. 14:13). It is our common tendency not to enjoy certain moments as much as we might otherwise because of the pervasive fear that they won't last; our lives will soon fall apart.

The world's joy depends on circumstances. The Christian's joy, if he has it, springs from God's presence in his life. The settled presence of God and a growing relationship with Jesus Christ can produce joy in the most difficult of circumstances.

Gil Beers tells of being at Forest Lawn in California and asking a mortician at that famous cemetery, "What was the most expensive funeral you ever had here?" Without batting an eye or having to search his memory, he told about a man who was so bitter at his former wife and children that he left them practically nothing in his will but assigned two hundred thousand dollars for his own ostentatious funeral. So a bronze casket was purchased for around eighteen thousand dollars and a beautiful rose window was put in place for twenty-five thousand dollars. After these and several other expenses were covered, the mortuary still had almost half the two hundred thousand dollars to spend. And how did they solve their problem? They bought one hundred thousand dollars worth of orchids. The funeral was attended by three people.

A lot of people live and die without any joy in their lives. They are embittered and angry for a lifetime. Then, as their legacy to the people who survive them, they want to impart something of that bitterness for them to have to bear.

Joy is a state of inward contentment and satisfaction that grows from a secure relationship with Jesus Christ. It is not dependent on the circumstances of the moment. Circumstances have a tendency to change. Joy, on the other hand, is something that defies circumstances and lifts its head in spite of difficult situations. Whereas the joy of this world is rather ephemeral and can come and go quickly, the joy which is given as a fruit of the presence of the Holy Spirit of God is a constant attitude.

As Tim Hansel says, joy is a posture, a position, a place.

> It is not a feeling; it is a *choice*. It is not based upon circumstances; it is based upon attitude. It is free, but it is not cheap. It is the by-product of a growing relationship with Jesus Christ. It is a promise, not a deal. It is available to us when we make ourselves available to him. It is something that we can receive by invitation and by choice. It requires commitment, courage, and endurance. . . .
>
> Pain is inevitable, but misery is optional. We cannot avoid pain, but we can avoid joy. God has given us such immense freedom that he will allow us to be as miserable as we want to be.
>
> I know some people who spend their entire lives practicing being unhappy, diligently pursuing joylessness. They get more mileage from having people feel sorry for them than from choosing to live out their lives in the context of joy (Tim Hansel. *You Gotta Keep Dancin'*. Elgin, IL: David C. Cook Publishing Co., 1985, pp. 54, 55).

Most of us understand joy as something we are going to experience as our circumstances improve. "When this has passed, I'm going to be happy." "When the kids are grown, you will see the real me come to the foreground." "When I get my career secured, you're going to see me involved in things of Christ." "When my braces come off, then you will find out how much fun I can be to have around."

If your strategy for joy involves constant deferment, forget it. You have already put off happiness so long that you may never experience it. You have chosen to avoid the wonderful responsibility of joy in the Spirit of God for the here and now in futile hope that it will rise up and strike you in the face somewhere down the road.

From a scriptural perspective, one discovers that joy comes to the people of God from some of the most surprising of circumstances. It is not a short-term fix related to something that can be bought. True joy has a price tag very different from dollars and cents. It is always free. And you won't have to move anywhere, go to school, find a mate, get out of debt, or die and go to heaven to find it. Joy is a gift God gives to anybody who will partake of it in the circumstance he or she is in right now. It has more to do with who you are than what you have, far more to do with healthiness of attitude than health of body.

There were once two men, both seriously ill, in the same small room of a great hospital. Quite a small room, just large enough for the pair of them—two beds, two bedside lockers, a door opening on the hall, and one window looking out on the world.

One of the men, as part of his treatment, was allowed to sit up in bed for an hour in the afternoon (something to do with draining the fluid from his lungs), and his bed was next to the window.

But the other man had to spend all his time flat on his back—and both of them had to be kept quiet and still. Which was the reason they were in the small room by themselves, and they were grateful for peace and privacy—none of the bustle and clatter and prying eyes of the general ward for them.

Of course, one of the disadvantages of their condition was that they weren't allowed to do much: no reading, no radio, certainly no television—they just had to keep quiet and still, just the two of them.

Well, they used to talk for hours and hours—about their wives, their children, their homes, their jobs, their hobbies, their childhood, what they did during the day, where they'd been on vacations—all that sort of thing. Every afternoon, when the man in the bed next to the window was propped up for his hour, he would pass the time by describing what he could see outside. And the other man began to live for those hours.

The window apparently overlooked a park, with a lake, where there were ducks and swans, children throwing them bread and sailing model boats, and young lovers walking hand in hand beneath the trees, and there were flowers and stretches of grass, games of softball, people taking their ease in the sunshine, and. right at the back, behind the fringe of trees, a fine view of the city skyline.

The man on his back would listen to all of this, enjoying every minute—how a child nearly fell into the lake, how beautiful the girls were in their summer dresses, then an exciting ball game, or a boy playing with his puppy. It got to the place that he could almost see what was happening outside.

Then one fine afternoon, when there was some sort of parade, the thought struck him: Why should the man next to the window have all the pleasure of seeing what was going on? Why shouldn't he get the chance?

He felt ashamed, and tried not to think like that, but the more he tried, the worse he wanted a change. He'd do anything!

In a few days, he had turned sour. He should be by the window. And he brooded, and couldn't sleep, and grew even more seriously ill—which none of the doctors understood.

One night as he stared at the ceiling, the other man suddenly woke up, coughing and choking, the fluid congesting in his lungs, his hands groping for the button that would bring the night nurse running. But the man watched without moving.

The coughing racked the darkness—on and on—choked off—then stopped—the sound of breathing stopped—and the man continued to stare at the ceiling.

In the morning the day nurse came in with water for their baths and found the other man dead. They took away his body, quietly, no fuss.

As soon as it seemed decent, the man asked if he could be moved to the bed next to the window. And they moved him, tucked

him in, and made him quite comfortable, and left him alone to
be quiet and still.

The minute they'd gone, he propped himself up on one elbow,
painfully and laboriously, and looked out the window.

It faced a blank wall (G. W. Target. "The Window" from *The
Window and Other Essays*. Mountain View, CA: Pacific Press
Publishing Association, 1973, pp. 5-7).

We have all known people like the first man, people whose
lives faced blank walls, but who could make them sound
beautiful. There was something inside them. Their joy with life
was contagious enough that we could draw strength from them
for our own struggles. We might have gone to cheer them up
in their hospital rooms or wheelchairs—only to come away
having received more encouragement than we gave.

But the second man illustrates the tendency of our sinful nature
to tie happiness to circumstances. He was so desperate for a
better set of conditions for himself that he was willing, in effect,
to kill for it. Only in the end did he realize that the other man's
joy was something he could never obtain by swapping places
with him. It was something inside that man and totally unrelated
to what was going on around him.

Joy Enhances the Total Person

A number of studies have been done lately which show that
positive attitudes toward life enable one to deal with things
constructively at every level of his being.

In his *Anatomy of an Illness*, Norman Cousins tells of his
personal experience in dealing with an illness (from which he
recovered in 1964) that was supposed to make him an invalid.
It tells how he countered the monsters of despair and hopelessness
with the guardian angels of joy and optimism. In a later book,
The Healing Heart, he writes of using the same strategy of joyful
affirmation toward life in coping with a heart attack he suffered
in 1980.

Scientists have picked up on Cousins' books and offered
physiological data which support his personal testimony. We

know, for example, that attitudes affect body chemistry. Depression appears to inhibit the body's ability to manufacture certain T-lymphocytes, white cells in the blood that identify and destroy abnormal (for example, cancer) cells. Optimism fosters the brain's production of noradrenaline, a neurotransmitter, which increases one's energy level and may help activate the complex immune system.

The psyche *does* have eyes. Physicians are increasingly aware of the contribution a patient's mental attitude makes to his total welfare. Families, friends, ministers, and social workers are being treated as team members to the healing process by growing numbers of health professionals.

No rational person is about to suggest that we substitute Three Stooges movies for penicillin or reruns of "Hogan's Heroes" for appendectomies. But many people from a variety of disciplines now believe that laughter, a positive outlook on life, and hope contribute their part—a very meaningful part—in fostering wellness.

The Bible says: "A cheerful heart is good medicine, but a crushed spirit dries up the bones" (Prov. 17:22).

Far more than its contribution to one's health and mental stability, however, joy is a staple of the genuinely spiritual life. Its presence in one's life means that his heart is in tune with God and filled by the Spirit. Joy, after all, is an element of the fruit of the Spirit, which distinguishes a believer's life from one who lives by the old, sinful nature.

What Cousins and the scientists who have studied the value of a positive and joyous attitude toward life have not told us is how to cultivate such a spirit. No humanistic approach to the problem can give a satisfactory answer, for joy which rises above one's circumstances is a spiritual phenomenon which requires a relationship with God through Jesus Christ.

A Christian's joy, cheerful heart, and pleasant disposition do not have to be at the whim of his circumstances. Since his reasons for rejoicing remain constant, even in difficult times, he can sing in a cell, praise God from his pain, and smile in the face of death. He can turn any sad place he visits into a house of God with the joy he radiates.

Where did we ever get the idea that Christianity required black suits and long faces? It just isn't so.

A Uniquely Christian Virtue

Joy is a uniquely Christian virtue. Paul writes: "Be joyful always" (1 Thess. 5:16).

The key word of the Epistle to the Philippians may very well be the word joy. As you thumb through it and look for the places in the epistle where the apostle speaks of joy and rejoicing, keep in mind the circumstances under which it was written. Philippians is one of four epistles preserved from Paul that we call "prison letters." During the two years Paul was at Rome under house arrest, from the spring of A.D. 60 to the spring of A.D. 62, he wrote this epistle about joy.

In the first chapter, he describes his reaction to some difficulties he was facing from his own brethren in Christ. Some people were preaching the gospel with renewed fervor at Rome out of a sense of jealousy and envy generated by Paul's presence. Perhaps they feared that their positions as leaders in the church were threatened by the fact that he had come to their city. Although they were increasing his personal burden by such petty behavior, here are Paul's words on the subject: "But what does it matter? The important thing is that in every way, whether from false motives or true, Christ is preached. And because of this I rejoice. Yes, and I will continue to rejoice" (Phil. 1:18). How easy is it for you to have that attitude when someone—especially a Christian who is supposed to be on your side in the struggle— works against you?

Go a chapter deeper into the book and you find Paul reflecting on his situation as a prisoner suffering for the work of Christ. "But even if I am being poured out like a drink offering on the sacrifice and service coming from your faith, I am glad and rejoice with all of you. So you too should be glad and rejoice with me" (2:17, 18). "It's okay that this is happening," he said. "Since I can accept it and rejoice over being allowed to suffer for the Lord, you should accept it and rejoice with me." What an attitude! No whining. No complaining about how unfair God had been with him. Just a sense of joy and security in the Lord.

Chapter 3 opens with these familiar words: "Finally, my brothers, rejoice in the LORD!" (Phil. 3:1a).

The fourth and final chapter says: "Rejoice in the Lord always. I will say it again: Rejoice!" (4:4).

"Joy" (Gk, *chairein* or *chairete*) was the word chosen out of the Greek vocabulary of the time as the characteristic greeting Christians would use when they passed each other on the streets. They would wave and say, "Joy to you!" They would smile and utter the single word, "Joy!"

Perhaps they picked it up from Jesus himself. When he appeared to the women running away from his empty tomb on the resurrection morning, he met them with the greeting, "Joy!" (Matt. 28:9, NKJV).

When the Jewish church settled the controversy over whether Gentiles were to be accepted into the fellowship of the churches of God, its leaders wrote a letter to the Gentile Christians. And the letter began: "Joy to the Gentile believers in Antioch, Syria and Cilicia!" (Acts 15:23).

James opened his little epistle to scattered, persecuted Christians who had been forced to flee from Jerusalem by writing: "Joy to the twelve tribes scattered among the nations" (James 1:1).

The New International Version translates the word in these three verses just cited with the English "Greetings." I don't quarrel with the idiomatic rendering here. It isn't incorrect. But it does not do justice to the nature and force of the greeting in question. Jesus didn't just greet and wave to the women that morning; he let them know that their sadness and confusion were over. "Let *joy* reign in your hearts," he told them, in effect, "for I am alive forever." The apostles and others responsible for drafting that letter to Gentile Christians were not just saying "Hello"; they were announcing the joyful news that the doors of the church have been swung open to everybody—without respect of persons. And James was not observing mere formality by opening his epistle to persecuted Christians with a greeting; he was urging them to feel good about God's ability to sustain them even in their trials and to rejoice.

Joy Is Secured in Christ

Joy is a state of inward contentment and satisfaction that grows out of a secure relationship with God. It is secured through the Son. Here are three passages which affirm this truth.

First, read this prayer of Paul for some of his beloved brothers and sisters in the faith.

> For this reason, since the day we heard about you, we have not stopped praying for you and asking God to fill you with the knowledge of his will through all spiritual wisdom and understanding. And we pray this in order that you may live a life worthy of the Lord and may please him in every way: bearing fruit in every good work, growing in the knowledge of God, being strengthened with all power according to his glorious might so that you may have great endurance and patience, and joyfully giving thanks to the Father, who has qualified you to share in the inheritance of the saints in the kingdom of light (Col. 1:9–12).

The problem in the church at Colossae was that some of the saints there had been turned aside to some form of this-worldly, pride-generating knowledge that came via the flesh and were neglecting the truth of the gospel. That is how the people of God lose their joy in every case. We turn our focus to all the wrong things. We think the circumstances have to be "just right" for us to have joy. So we try to climb the world's ladder to success through achieving and having, forgetting in the process that greatness in Christ comes by being a servant.

Thus, Paul prayed for them to have "spiritual wisdom and understanding" and to "live a life worthy of the Lord." Living that way, and "bearing fruit in every good work," they would be able to give thanks to God *joyfully* for what he was doing in their lives.

Second, there is the statement from Paul we have already bumped into in this book:

> For the kingdom of God is not a matter of eating and drinking, but of righteousness, peace and joy in the Holy Spirit, because anyone who serves Christ in this way is pleasing to God and approved by men (Rom. 14:17, 18).

What is the kingdom of God to you? Bus routes through the neighborhood? New audiovisual equipment in the classrooms? New carpet in the auditorium? A full house every Sunday? Contribution figures larger than the church three blocks away to show that your church is doing better than theirs?

The kingdom of God is *not* circumstances. It is something happening in you by the power of God. It is his reign over your mind, personality, abilities, and total being. And it is, in part, the joy which he builds into you by the presence of his indwelling Spirit. The kingdom of God is right living in this wicked world because of the love of God you have in your heart as a motivation for doing his will; it is peace in a world torn with conflict and turmoil; it is joy in a world that cannot find happiness in all the pleasures and creature comforts it pursues and lavishes on itself.

Righteousness, peace, and joy result from the fruitful presence of the Spirit of God in you. No, you cannot make yourself be happy and joyous under difficult circumstances. You can't lift yourself by your bootstraps and smile in the face of adversity. But the Spirit of God can generate joy—settled contentment and brightness of spirit—by his presence in you. Joy is a gift rather than an accomplishment, a fruit of the Spirit and not a work of the flesh.

Third, go to the Gospels and read the words of Jesus from his farewell discourse to the apostles. Since these are among the last statements they heard from his lips before the cross, they must be significant.

> As the Father has loved me, so have I loved you. Now remain in my love. If you obey my commands, you will remain in my love, just as I have obeyed my Father's commands and remain in his love. I have told you this so that my joy may be in you and that your joy may be complete (John 15:9-11).

Do you know why Jesus was able to keep smiling through everything he faced? Do you know how he was able to see the cross just ahead and not wince? There is no secret to it. Step one: *He was secure in his Father's love.* He loved the Father, and the Father loved him. Step two: *He obeyed the Father within the security of love.* Step three: *He experienced and shared joy.*

Love is the first item named in connection with the fruit of the Spirit. That is not coincidental. Just as Jesus grounded everything on love in his life, so must we ground all things in love in our lives. Love produces obedience, and obedience generates joy—the joy of a clear conscience, the joy of a surrendered lifestyle, the joy of blessing others.

"You may have my joy," said Jesus, in effect. "Live within the security of his love as I have and give yourself to him in the

same yielded obedience you have witnessed in my life, and you
will experience the same joy I know—even if it should cost you
as much as it is costing me to embrace such a pattern for living."

Conclusion

It is a contradiction to talk about a joyless Christian. A joyless
life just isn't a Christian life. Christians have reasons in abundance
to rejoice, be happy, know joy.

To know Christ is to experience joy in having one's sins
forgiven, in being able to share the good news of forgiveness
with other people, in healing broken fellowships, in bearing
burdens, in doing good. And, yes, it is to experience suffering,
if need be, for the sake of the Lord Jesus Christ. Through it
all, there is joy—joy *larger* than your life circumstances, joy that
doesn't depend on what is happening around you, but which
rises above those things.

The fruit of the Spirit is *joy*.

5

Peace

The Spirit of God has been given to those who are children of God for the purpose of bearing fruit in our lives. His presence serves, not to overpower our resisting wills, but to empower our submissive souls. And one of the sure signs of his effective work in any believer's experience is the possession of unshakable *peace*.

Peace is an enigmatic quality among Christian virtues.

Jesus is the Prince of Peace. Yet, as he said himself, his coming into the world produced not peace but a sword (Matt. 10:34). Since he was light, everything that partook of darkness was disturbed by his presence. Since he was truth, everything that was a lie or which was founded on a lie stood in opposition to him. Since he was altogether good, every person who loved evil hated his presence.

Jesus predicted that his followers would experience some of the same opposition and hatred he had known before them. He said, "If the world hates you, keep in mind that it hated me first. . . . They will treat you this way because of my name, for they do not know the One who sent me" (John 15:18, 21).

At a time when he was tasting fierce antagonism and warning his followers of the same, Jesus was, nevertheless, at peace within himself. And he promised to give peace to those who would follow him. "I have told you these things, so that in me you

may have peace," he said. ". . . In this world you will have trouble.
But take heart! I have overcome the world" (John 16:33).

This talk of peace in the midst of so much opposition and
pain is what makes me say that peace is an enigma among
Christian virtues. Constantly besieged by enemies and animosity,
Jesus tells us, "If you choose to follow me, you're buying into
the same thing." Yet he says, "I am at peace and will give you
my peace." In the same breath he says, "In the world you're going
to have trouble, but I'm going to give you peace, nonetheless."

Happiness and Happenings

We are inclined to tie peace to circumstances—and we are
mistaken in doing so. Peace is larger than circumstances and
independent of them. Most of us are tyrannized by circumstances.
We think that whatever is happening *around* us is destined to
determine what will go on *inside* us. Jesus says: "It isn't so. Things
happening all around you may be turbulent, painful, and trouble-
some, but I will give you peace."

When the birth of Jesus was announced, angels told the
shepherds that his coming would mean this: "and on earth peace
to men on whom God's favor rests" (Luke 2:14b). What is often
called the "Christian message" is the mistaken notion that Jesus
came to put the world at peace, to end conflict among nations,
to secure an end to all hostilities. Based on the inaccurate
translation of the King James Version at Luke 2:14, a wrong-
headed idea of what Jesus came to give men persists still. He
did not bring a peace package for the Middle East, Central
America, and Southeast Asia. He came with an offer of peace
to anxious individuals in all parts of the world, a peace which
would be independent of whatever political, economic, or social
stresses they might be facing.

All through his life, Jesus clearly seems to have been at peace.
You never see him in a panic. You never catch him exhibiting
the signs of nervous anxiety that are so common to my experience
and, perhaps, to yours. It is laughable to try to picture Jesus
wringing his hands, biting his nails, and chewing his lip as he
tried to figure out how to respond to a situation.

Jesus had a settled, peaceful spirit throughout his time in the
flesh. Incredibly, he was the only one who figured in his death

scene who was at peace. Confused disciples were fleeing, denying, and hiding. Wicked enemies were lying, playing power politics, and denying justice. Innocent bystanders were bewildered and confused by it all. In the middle of all this confusion and horror, the Son of Man was restrained and composed; he even prayed, "Father, forgive them, for they do not know what they are doing" (Luke 23:34).

Angels sang of peace at his birth, yet his entire life—from cradle to grave—was hounded with strife. Even in the context of an unjust death, he remained fully at peace. Through it all he promised both stress and peace to those who would live in him and let his Spirit live in them.

You and I can know, live, and make peace only as Jesus did— as a state of inner serenity given by God alone. The kingdom of God, Paul reminds us, is not externals—such as eating and drinking—but internal qualities of righteousness, peace, and joy in the Holy Spirit (Rom. 14:17).

Peace with God

In order to understand and have peace in Christian experience, one has to begin with the issue of peace with God. There is no peace *of* God in one's life until he or she is at peace *with* God. "Therefore, since we have been justified through faith, we have peace with God through our Lord Jesus Christ" (v. 5:1).

One receives the Prince of Peace in obeying the gospel of peace and by embracing a life of peace. This is not to say that a Christian's life will be at peace with evil, at peace with lies, at peace with hypocrisy. It certainly does not mean that one will be at peace with the sinful environment in which he lives, for it will always remain an alien environment to the Christian. Peace with God very often requires one to be at war with evil deeds and evil people. But I reiterate that peace with God is an internal phenomenon, one which is not determined by circumstances. It is a peace built on the foundation of faith.

Isaiah made the same link between faith and peace that Paul did. He wrote:

> You will keep in perfect peace
> him whose mind is steadfast,
> because he trusts in you. (Isa. 26:3).

Peace is God's gift to the one whose mind is steadfast in its trusting faith in him.

The reason the Old Testament covenant people never fully experienced the peace God wanted to give them lay in their unbelief. That is not my harsh judgment, but the matter-of-fact statement of the Word of God. Thousands who perished in the wilderness wanderings were unable to enter divine rest "because of their unbelief" (Heb. 3:19). The same writer adds: "It still remains that some will enter that rest, and those who formerly had the gospel preached to them did not go in, because of their disobedience" (4:6).

Unbelief and disobedience thwart peace with God. You cannot have peace with heaven while living in rebellion against the divine will. You certainly cannot know peace while you are living to the flesh and giving way to evil desires.

In the three verses immediately prior to the text which speaks of the fruit of the Spirit, Paul lists what he calls "acts of the sinful nature." The list includes such things as fornication, drunkenness, strife, and envy (Gal. 5:19-21). Nobody who lives that way is at peace. You may be able to testify to the truth of that out of your personal experience.

There is no sense of peace with God for the man or woman who is cultivating a sinful nature. There is a powerful (and sometimes overbearing) sense of guilt. There is intense conflict. There is strife with family, business partners, or the law. There is everything else but peace. Peace comes through faith in God, reorienting one's life from the works of the flesh to Jesus Christ, and obeying the gospel of peace.

Peace Within Self

Peace with God relates directly to one's ability to be at peace with himself. In the Sermon on the Mount, Jesus stressed this truth in a most powerful way. He attacked worry and what worry means about one's faith (that is, trust) in God.

Worry is a part of the unsettledness that comes of living to gratify the desires of the sinful nature. "So do not worry, saying, 'What shall we eat?' or 'What shall we drink?' or 'What shall we wear?'" said Jesus, "for the pagans run after all these things, and your heavenly Father knows that you need them" (Matt.

6:31, 32). One who is at peace with God knows that all his needs are known to a faithful Father in heaven.

People who do not believe in God run around trying to satisfy their needs by their own devices. They try to find not only clothing and shelter, but happiness and meaning in life by the only methods they know—methods which relate to the flesh, carnal man, and a sinful nature. They seek the good life by the acts of the sinful nature—and are confused, frustrated, and lost. They cry out in the pain of a meaningless existence.

You probably know the basic life story of David. At one point in his life, David was being pursued by his son Absalom and his supporters. They were attempting a coup against David and wanted to replace him on the throne with rebellious and sinful Absalom. Under this painful and threatening circumstance, David wrote:

> O LORD, how many are my foes!
> How many rise up against me!
> Many are saying of me,
> "God will not deliver him" (Ps. 3:1, 2).

With the externals of his life in chaos, a trusting David was not tyrannized by those circumstances. When everyone else had given up his situation as hopeless, this was his attitude:

> But you are a shield around me, O LORD;
> my Glorious One who lifts up my head.
> To the LORD I cry aloud,
> and he answers me from his holy hill.
>
> I lie down and sleep;
> I wake again because the LORD sustains me.
> I will not fear the tens of thousands
> drawn up against me on every side (Ps. 3:3–6).

Be honest. Do you ever have trouble sleeping? I've had some long nights. I know what that does to the way I feel, to the way I am able to handle responsibility, and to the way I relate to other people. It can happen to anyone. You get into a financial strain or a career difficulty; there is a problem in the marriage or trouble with one of the children; there is an enemy rising up against you or telling a lie about you—so you don't sleep.

David knew what it does to someone to have those things happening in his life. His son was leading an insurrection against him; thousands were set against his position as king; nobody thought God could deliver him. But every night he went to bed and slept peacefully!

What would you have done if you had been in David's situation? Would you have been tyrannized by the circumstances? I think I might have been. David said, "I lie down, and *I go to sleep!* I wake again, because the LORD sustains me" (v. 5, italics added).

What is the secret to that sort of peace? There is a New Testament passage which is crucial to the subject. Read it carefully.

> Do not be anxious about anything, but in everything, by prayer and petition, with thanksgiving, present your requests to God. And the peace of God, which transcends all understanding, will guard your hearts and your minds in Christ Jesus (Phil. 4:6-7).

In one of the most practical examinations of this text I have ever read, the late D. Martyn Lloyd-Jones provides some helpful insights into the meaning of these two verses in his excellent book *Spiritual Depression*.

First, there is the familiar negative you can hear from a friendly neighbor, "Don't worry. Do not be anxious about anything." We have all received that advice without being told what to put in the place of our worry. As a Christian, have you ever had that guilty feeling which comes because the preacher has gone on about how Christians aren't supposed to worry? Then, because you have gone home still worried, you think that maybe you aren't a genuine Christian at all. So, worry at one level is compounded with worry on another level. The cycle can become vicious.

Second, Paul balances the negative injunction against worry with a positive plan for replacing it with something better. Here is the plan: "In everything, by prayer and petition, with thankgiving, present your requests to God." Thinking back to the Sermon on the Mount, this is basically a reformulation of what Jesus said: "Pagans worry. Christians trust."

There are three steps to the plan Paul outlines for overcoming worry.

Step One: *Pray.*

... never does the apostle say that if we pray, our prayer in and of itself will make us feel better. It is a disgraceful thing that people should pray for that reason. ... Prayer is not auto-suggestion.

Neither does he say: "Pray, because while you are praying you will not be thinking about that problem, and therefore you will have temporary relief". ...

Neither does he say, and I say this advisedly: "Pray, because prayer changes things." No, it does not. Prayer does not "change things". ... What the apostle says is this: "You pray and make your requests known unto God, and God will do something." It is not your prayer that is going to do it, it is not you who are going to do it, but God (D. Martyn Lloyd-Jones. *Spiritual Depression: Its Causes and Its Cures.* Grand Rapids: Wm. B. Eerdmans Publishing Company, 1965, pp. 269-270).

Prayer in a Christian's experience begins with praising God, acknowledging God. It is coming before God to praise him for who he is and for what he has done to give you peace with him through Christ. You will soon get to the external circumstances of your life that are troubling you, but always start every prayer with praising God's name and faithfulness. Forget for a moment that there are some situations which are less than peaceful with your wife, with your children, with a boss, with a neighbor. "God, I thank you that I'm at peace with you." Start there.

On those nights when you cannot sleep, start praying. And as you begin, don't start the prayer with your problems. Start with God, and glorify him for who he is and for the relationship you have with him.

Step Two: *Petition.*

Now that you have offered praise to him, let God know what is worrying you and spoiling your sleep, your work, your relationships, your spiritual life. Tell him what he already knows, but do it with your own lips. "God, this is why I'm not sleeping at night. God, this is why I've lost my appetite. God, this is why I'm so grouchy with everybody. God, this is why I feel like my very spiritual life is falling apart. But, God, because I have praised you and acknowledged you as my God, I commit those things to you in the confidence that you are the only one who can resolve them."

When we pray and commit our anxieties to God, he will do something. To a non-Christian, prayer probably appears to be nothing more than catharsis, autosuggestion, or filling one's mind with reflections to crowd out the bad thoughts. For those who understand God, prayer is nothing of the sort. For them, prayer is offered with the confidence that the God to whom they are praying will change their lives, not that their act of praying will change anything. Thus he is praised because of his power; exalted because of his holiness; trusted because of his faithfulness. We petition him in the confidence that he can handle what we cannot.

Step Three: *Give thanks.*

Give thanks for what? Give thanks for everything you can think of to name that is good in your life. Give God thanks for hearing the petitions you have just laid before him and that you are now trusting him to resolve.

As the Spirit moved him to write it, Paul gave us this three-step plan for dealing with our anxieties—and this promise: "And the peace of God, which transcends all understanding, will guard your hearts and your minds in Christ Jesus" (Phil. 4:7). The word *guard* here means to garrison, wall about, keep one from being under the tyranny of external things. No matter what continues to happen on the outside, God will give peace to the person who handles his anxieties this way. With you and God garrisoned together, the enemy on the outside cannot conquer you.

Someone may say, "I wish it were that simple." It really is! I didn't believe it for years, and prayer was about as important to me as it seems to be to other Christians who have talked with me about their prayer lives. So we stew and our stomachs churn; our heads ache and we don't sleep; we feel guilty because we cannot obey the injunction against worrying. You will keep on worrying unless you learn to approach problems in the positive way of prayer, petition, and thanksgiving—in that order.

Peace with Others

At peace with God and within your own heart, you can then begin to experience peace at the level of relationships with other people.

God wants his church united, at peace, and free from internal rivalries. "Make every effort to keep the unity of the Spirit through the bond of peace" (Eph. 4:3). "Let the peace of Christ rule in your hearts, since, as members of one body, you were called to peace . . ." (Col. 3:15).

At the level of the local church, peace is God's way of relating brothers and sisters to one another. In the church I have been with for almost a decade, I can honestly say there has not been a single disruptive situation to arise, to threaten unity, to rend the fabric of the body. I have worked in church settings in the past, however, where one brushfire after another had to be stamped out. Sometimes a prairie fire would destroy peace and blacken the spiritual landscape.

At the larger level of intercongregational relationships and brotherhood relationships, God demands oneness. The power of Satan to stir up the sinful nature of believers often defeats the divine agenda. Newspapers which sow discord, preachers who function out of rivalry and jealousy, and competition among congregations indicate that the peace of God is lacking. God wants us to be at peace rather than going for the jugular, to keep unity rather than act as watchdogs over each other's faith, and to build up the total body of Christ rather than build armed camps whose responsibilities are to fight one another constantly.

"But isn't the imagery of soldiers fighting a biblical metaphor for the church?" one asks. It is a biblical metaphor for how the church relates to a sinful and unbelieving world. It is not a biblical picture for the way the church lives out its brother-to-brother relationships.

Peace is missing from the hearts of some who misunderstand our role in relation to our brethren. The progression is: *peace with God, peace with self,* and then, *peace with others.* And if either of the first two is missing, the third can never come.

The Bible also challenges Christ's disciples to be at peace with all men, not only with one another. "Make every effort to live in peace with all men and to be holy" (Heb. 12:14a). Sometimes the requirement to be holy will have to take precedence over the goal of being at peace with all men. Often, however, the failure to be at peace is over something far less crucial than an issue of holiness. Here is a statement of the matter which is totally realistic: "If it is possible, as far as it depends on you, live at peace with everyone" (Rom. 12:18).

When you are not at peace with people in the world or with another brother, make sure it is not your fault. If you have done wrong, repent of it; at that point the burden is no longer on you but on him—to forgive. If you have offended someone, apologize; your obligation is not to defend your pride but to maintain peace. If there has been a misunderstanding, make the first move to talk things over with the other party; God made the first move to get through to you.

The reason it is so difficult for most of us to be at peace with the folks around us—whether brethren or unbelievers— is that we have not embraced the key to peace: *vulnerability*.

> Often we fail to have peace with other people simply because we feel threatened by them. Our natural reaction when we are threatened is to build defenses, barriers between ourselves and the source of the threat. Once we have defenses, we naturally assume a defensive attitude.
>
> If there are barriers between me and another person, I don't solve the problem by attacking his defenses. I approach it by tearing down my own defenses. I make myself vulnerable. One of the reasons peace is not restored in many relationships is simply this: We want others to lower their defenses before we do anything about ours. *If I lower my guard*, we reason, *he'll get me*. This is the crux of the matter. This is the heart of the peacemaker who is willing to pay the price for peace (D. Stuart Briscoe. *Tough Truths for Today's Living*. Waco, TX: Word Books, 1978, pp. 44, 45).

Are you thinking: "That doesn't make sense. That stands everything I've ever been taught on its head"? Kingdom counsel stands everything the world believes on its head. It seems that in nation-to-nation relationships the only way to peace is through strength. You have to build a large enough arsenal of weapons that your enemy will know it is going to cost him more than he can possibly hope to gain if he comes against you. But the kingdom of God has to do with one-to-one relationships among believers and with non-Christian neighbors, and it does not function by that model.

In personal relationships the only way to peace is by turning the other cheek. The only way to peace is by giving up more than you have been asked to give up. The only way to peace is to be vulnerable.

Jesus is our perfect paradigm in peacemaking. How did he

make peace? It cost him the shedding of his blood. God has reconciled the world to himself through Christ, "by making peace through his blood, shed on the cross" (Col. 1:20). Jesus made peace by being vulnerable to the point of death. Insisting that peace can be had only when you have overwhelmed and defeated someone, when he admits he is wrong and you are right, when he bows and scrapes at your feet—that is the way of the world and contrary to the kingdom of God. Life in the kingdom allows you to accept more responsibility than you are due to take. Because you are at peace with God and self, you are secure enough that you can be vulnerable to another human being. You can make the first move. You can say, "I was wrong. I am sorry. I will do anything to make things right."

In things of this nature, it is often the case that little children can lead us. Remember what Jesus said about becoming as a little child in order to share in the kingdom of heaven?

Robert Coles is a psychiatrist at Harvard University. In 1960 he was living in New Orleans, when the public schools of that city were desegregated. Three little black girls enrolled in the first grade in one public school and another black girl enrolled in the first grade at William T. Frantz School. She had to be escorted to and from school by federal marshals, because the city police would not protect her. Coles thought her experience would make an interesting study and could be the basis for writing a good paper to present to the American Psychiatric Association. So when Ruby Bridges enrolled in school at age six, Coles started his study.

Dr. Coles visited with Ruby and her family twice a week. He asked her how she was doing and always got polite "I'm okay" responses. Her mother assured the psychiatrist, "She's doing fine."

Unable to believe that a child under such stress could be handling things that well, Coles pressed for information about sleep habits, appetite, and relationships with other children in the neighborhood. Ruby was sleeping soundly each night, eating well, and playing with the children in her neighborhood as before. Even her first-grade teacher told Dr. Coles, "You know, I don't understand this child. She seems so happy. She comes here so cheerfully."

It just didn't make sense. Here was a child being taunted daily by adults. About fifty people were there every morning as she came to school under special escort. Another fifty or seventy-five showed up every afternoon as she was leaving school. They called her ugly names. They told her they did not want her at the school. They told her they were going to kill her. An incident occurred one day which put things in new perspective.

Ruby's school teacher told Dr. Coles, "I saw Ruby talking to those people on the street this morning. She stopped and seemed to be talking to the people in the street." Here is the psychiatrist's account of what he learned in following up on the "conversation" that day.

We went to Ruby's home that night, and I asked her, "Ruby, how was your day today?"
She said, "It was okay."
"I was talking to your teacher today and she told me that she asked you about something when you came into school early in the morning."
"I don't remember," Ruby said.
"Your teacher told me that she saw you talking to people in the street."
"Oh, yes. I told her I wasn't talking to them. I was just saying a prayer for them."
"Ruby, you pray for the people there?"
"Oh, yes."
"Really?"
"Yes."
I said, "Why do you do that?"
"Because they need praying for," she answered.
"Do they?"
"Oh, yes."
"Ruby, why do you think they need you to pray for them?"
"Because I should."
"Why?"
"Because I should."
Then Ruby's mother came into the room. She had heard this line of inquiry, and she said, "We tell Ruby that it's important that she pray for the people." She said Ruby had the people on a list and prayed for them at night.
I said, "You do, Ruby, you pray for them at night, too?"
"Oh, yes."
"Why do you do that?"
"Well, because they need praying for."

Once, a couple of weeks after the first time I mentioned it, I again asked Ruby about this praying. "Ruby, I'm still puzzled. I'm trying to figure out why you think you should be the one to pray for such people, given what they do to you twice a day, five days a week."
"Well," she said, "especially it should be me."
"Why you especially?"
"Because if you're going through what they're doing to you, you're the one who should be praying for them." And then she quoted to me what she had heard in church. The minister said that Jesus went through a lot of trouble, and he said about the people who were causing the trouble, "Forgive them, because they don't know what they're doing." And now little Ruby was saying this in the 1960s about the people in the streets of New Orleans (Robert Coles. "The Inexplicable Prayers of Ruby Bridges," *Princeton Seminary Bulletin* 5; 1, New Series, Nov. 1984).

I wonder if this true story could have anything to do with why Jesus said, "Of such is the kingdom of heaven."

Praying for one's enemies is not the natural way we human beings react to threats. The natural response is not to get on our knees and pray for them. It is to strike back, to put them in their place, to call them something equally insulting, to get even. A person at peace with God and with himself can learn to be at peace with other people. "Of such is the kingdom of heaven." Those people may always be his enemies. They may never change. Through prayer, petition, and thanksgiving, however, his heart can be so garrisoned by God that he can be at peace rather than tyrannized by those circumstances. The popular notion is that peace comes through the elimination of conflict, but the truth is that it comes only through pain and vulnerability and tears—and sometimes even the shedding of blood.

Conclusion

In the context of encouraging some Christians who were in jeopardy before their persecutors, the apostle to the Jews quoted from an Old Testament psalm:

> Whoever would love life
> and see good days

> must keep his tongue from evil
>   and his lips from deceitful speech.
> He must turn from evil and do good;
>   *he must seek peace and pursue it.*
> For the eyes of the Lord are on the righteous,
>   and his ears are attentive to their prayer,
> but the face of the Lord is against those
>   who do evil (1 Peter 3:10–12, italics added).

"He must seek peace and pursue it." But he must pursue peace in the power of the Spirit, and not in the frailty of the flesh, or it can never come. With the Spirit of God as the internal dynamic to give you peace, you can "live in peace. And the God of love and peace will be with you" (2 Cor. 13:11). It doesn't matter what is going on in your life. It doesn't matter how turbulent circumstances are or how tyrannized you are by them. God can give you peace.

And if the people of God come to be a people of peace, we will have a testimony to the world that will be more effective in getting them to listen to the gospel than our loud sermons and bombastic declarations. The gentle peace of a heart fixed on the Father, cleansed by the Son, and inhabited by the Spirit, allows one to be a force for peace in a world which is daily tearing itself apart.

The fruit of the Spirit is *peace.*

6
Patience

To write of *patience* makes me feel hypocritical. I joke about my impatience—the same way most of us make light of things that embarrass us and make us feel personally uncomfortable.

We live in an era of instant gratification. In our demand for instant results, we constantly court instant disaster. Not only have most of us left our rural and agrarian roots behind, but also our understanding of the fact that things happen best on the model of cultivation, planting, a season of gradual growth, and ultimate harvest. I want to plant and reap in the same day. We believers want to receive God's Spirit when we are born anew and skip over spiritual infancy and adolescence into mature faith. It just doesn't work that way.

The spirit of our impatient age is epitomized in a purely hypothetical but altogether believable scenario: John Doe comes in from work and sits down to a cup of instant coffee and a TV dinner. He eats in a rush in order to leave his house, jump on the rapid transit system his community built a few years back, and get to a seminar on "How to Be Successful Overnight." Back at home later in the evening, he discovers he is so worked up that he must take a sleeping pill so he can fall asleep fast, with two aspirin on the side to ward off the slight headache which threatens to disrupt his sleep.

The next morning he has instant breakfast drink and a toaster waffle before going off to work. There he demands immediate competence from a new employee and barks at her for not understanding on first explanation the complex tasks that she has been hired to perform.

In midafternoon, he experiences a bit of a letdown as his energy begins to fade. Someone offers him a snort of cocaine, describing the instant sense of exhiliration and energy that comes from it, and assists him in beginning a life-destroying habit.

At home that evening, he and his wife only pass each other with a gruff word or two. Because the atmosphere is tense, he excuses himself quickly and goes to a bar in order to have a drink and unwind from the day's tensions. There he strikes up a conversation with a woman he has never met before and winds up spending the night in a motel room with a total stranger because it promises instant gratification.

This hypothetical case study would be almost humorous except for its obvious correspondence to the life situation of so many people. The fewer details which have to be altered to make the story fit your situation, the more trouble you are in.

In spite of the fact that we refuse to tolerate pain, offense, delay, and incompetence, the Bible still tells us that we are obliged to pursue, nurture, and exhibit patience. God calls us to be patient with people and circumstances, to wait for his purposes to unfold.

> Yet the LORD longs to be gracious to you;
>   he rises to show you compassion.
> For the LORD is a God of justice.
> Blessed are all those who will wait for him! (Isa. 30:18).

For the grace of God that brings salvation has appeared to all men. It teaches us to say 'No' to ungodliness and worldly passions, and to live self-controlled, upright and godly lives in this present age, while we wait for the blessed hope—the glorious appearing of our great God and Savior, Jesus Christ, who gave himself for us to redeem us from all wickedness and to purify for himself a people that are his very own, eager to do what is good (Titus 2:11-14).

God asks us to wait, to be long-suffering, and to realize that not every need can be met instantly. Miracles have only rarely been used by God to achieve his will. Most often his answer to our requests is: "Trust me—and wait. Be patient as I rise to meet your need in my own way and in my own time."

What Is Patience?

The word translated "patience" in the text of Galatians 5:22–23 is *makrothymia*. A compound word, it joins the Greek term for "large, big, grand" (*makros*) with the word for "emotions, anger, rage" (*thymos*). The resulting term refers to the ability to contain and hold in check large quantities of emotion, such as anger or frustration.

The biblical idea is not simply that one must suppress his feelings and seethe with anger, but that he should do something to deal with them before they explode and harm him and those near him. The concept inherent in the word implies "long-temperedness" as opposed to being short-tempered. The word is sometimes translated into English with our term "long-suffering," a more precise equivalent for the Greek word used in this passage. To suffer a long time with a wayward person or painful situation stands in sharp contrast to bailing out on people and circumstances which do not lend themselves to a quick fix.

There are other words in the Greek New Testament which come into English as *patience*. Some of them are rather aggressive terms. *Hupomonē*, for example, usually seems to carry the idea of pushing back against a situation in order to handle its stresses and deal with its demands.

The word *makrothymia*, on the other hand, is generally tinged with a note of restraint and resignation, even passivity. It seems to recognize that sometimes there is no identifiable place to push back, no "handle" to grab in order to cope with a situation. It implies a willingness to wait. Accepting the fact that not every problem has an instant cure and not every desire has an instant gratification, one must suffer long and wait with patience for God to open a door of deliverance.

Makrothymia is used in the Septuagint to translate a Hebrew phrase meaning "slow to anger." Numbers 14:18a attributes this quality to Yahweh: "The LORD is slow to anger, abounding in love and forgiving sin and rebellion." One finds the same word used later in the Old Testament in Psalm 86:15:

> But you, O LORD, are a compassionate
> and gracious God,
> slow to anger, abounding in love
> and faithfulness.

How glad I am that our God isn't short-fused. If he were an impatient God, he would have destroyed me long ago. He has had to travel with me down many a fascinating sidetrack to righteousness and holiness. He has had to be patient with me far beyond the limit I would have gone for someone else. Perhaps you could testify to the same sense of gratitude for God's long-suffering.

The Old Testament not only points to and praises patience as a quality in God, it also commends it as a trait for wise and godly people to exhibit to one another. Here are two proverbs collected by Solomon on this point: "A patient man has great understanding, but a quick-tempered man displays folly" (Prov. 14:29) and "Better a patient man than a warrior, a man who controls his temper than one who takes a city" (16:32). Understanding the Hebrew literary device known as parallelism, one reads these proverbs and knows immediately what qualities are being singled out for praise. The former puts a "quick-tempered man" as the antithesis to the "patient man"; the latter parallels "a man who controls his temper" with a "patient man."

Being quick-tempered and volatile is a mark of the sinful nature. Having the sort of disposition that is best likened to dry powder looking for a match is a work of the flesh. The ability to be slow to anger, to have a long fuse, and to suffer with unpleasantness for a long time is the result of the Spirit's presence and work in the life of a godly person.

Coming to the New Testament, *makrothymia* is used in several different settings to describe God and the lovely character that makes us desire him. Paul asks: "Or do you show contempt for the riches of his kindness, tolerance and patience, not realizing that God's kindness leads you towards repentance?" (Rom. 2:4). Look closely at the three words which are clustered here: *kindness, tolerance,* and *patience.* Because God possesses such a disposition, he has a long fuse and is slow to anger.

Then there is the familiar statement of 2 Peter 3:9. Peter affirms: "God is not slow in keeping his promise, as some understand slowness. He is patient with you, not wanting anyone to perish, but everyone to come to repentance." It isn't that God doesn't take note of the wicked things we do on planet Earth. He just reacts differently to provocation than we do. God is patient. God is waiting with restraint. He is giving us time to repent.

The New Testament also exhorts us to imitate this godly quality of patience. Against the frustrations he was facing in trying to preach the gospel to recalcitrant people, Timothy was encouraged: "Preach the Word; be prepared in season and out of season; correct, rebuke and encourage—with great patience and careful instruction" (2 Tim. 4:2). This is still good counsel to preachers young or old. We tend to be so impatient as teachers. We wrestle with the Word for years, believe we have discerned some important truth, and mount the pulpit to proclaim it. Then we may sit in harsh judgment on any who do not see, after one presentation, what we searched for over years of diligence. That is an act of the sinful nature. Under the control of the Spirit of God, one is able to preach, correct, rebuke, and encourage—all with great patience.

Hebrews 6:12 is a passage which exhorts all Christians and not just their teachers. The writer urges: "We do not want you to become lazy, but to imitate those who through faith and patience inherit what has been promised."

God's Patience and Our Own

There is a parable known to most of us as the Parable of the Unmerciful Servant. It could as easily be titled the Parable of the *Impatient* Servant.

> Therefore the kingdom of heaven is like a king who wanted to settle accounts with his servants. As he began the settlement, a man who owed him ten thousand talents was brought to him. Since he was not able to pay, the master ordered that he and his wife and his children and all that he had be sold to repay the debt.
>
> The servant fell on his knees before him. "Be patient with me," he begged, "and I will pay back everything." The servant's master took pity on him, canceled the debt and let him go.
>
> But when that servant went out, he found one of his fellow servants who owed him a hundred denarii. He grabbed him and began

to choke him. "Pay back what you owe me!" he demanded.

His fellow servant fell to his knees and begged him, "Be patient with me, and I will pay you back."

But he refused. Instead, he went off and had the man thrown into prison until he could pay the debt. When the other servants saw what had happened, they were greatly distressed and went and told their master everything that had happened.

Then the master called the servant in. "You wicked servant," he said, "I canceled all that debt of yours because you begged me to. Shouldn't you have had mercy on your fellow servant just as I had on you?" In anger his master turned him over to the jailers until he should pay back all he owed.

This is how my heavenly Father will treat each of you unless you forgive your brother from your heart (Matt. 18:23–35).

Notice that the servant implored his king, "Be *patient* with me" (v. 26). Then, when the forgiven servant was approached by a fellow servant who owed him a paltry sum by comparison, he was begged, "Be *patient* with me" (v. 29, italics added). He asked for and received patience—and cancellation of his debt; he refused to show patience to another—and fell under heavy judgment for his failure.

If God has demonstrated patience with you, how dare you not show some patience with others? Divine and human patience are due to go hand in hand. One who has experienced the former ought to be willing to bestow the latter. Against the background of divine slowness to anger, "long-fusedness," and patience, it hardly seems appropriate for us to bark at and threaten one another—whether mate, child, parent, employee, or brother in Christ. Unless we are patient and merciful, God will eventually withhold his patience and mercy from us. This is the old pattern of reaping what one sows.

The context of the Parable of the Unmerciful/Impatient Servant makes the story even more impressive. Peter had just raised the question: "LORD, how many times shall I forgive my brother when he sins against me? Up to seven times?" (Matt. 18:21). Jesus' answer to his frequently impetuous disciple was this: "I tell you, not seven times, but seventy-seven times" (v. 22). The point of his answer was not to limit forgiveness and merciful conduct with the number he used. To the contrary, the point is that there is not to be a limit placed on forgiveness. Since love "keeps no record of wrongs" (1 Cor. 13:5b), one can never know for sure that he has reached an outer limit of 77 episodes of forgiveness; thus, his obligation is to forgive as often as there is any evidence of need for it.

In a still larger context, look as far back in Matthew 18 as the fifteenth verse. There Jesus begins explaining how to deal with offenses involving brethren. He outlines a procedure that begins with personal contact between the two estranged parties, brings in other caring individuals who might be helpful, and, ultimately, can go before a whole church. The point of all this is driven home with a story about being patient with one's fellow servants.

Most of us are prone to look for someone to back us up in being hateful and spiteful when we have been wronged. If John mistreats Bob, what Bob may want more than anything else is for Dick to tell him to respond in kind. If Mary wounds Beth with her tongue, Beth just might fire right back—and then turn to Sherry to hear, "That's just what I'd have done, and I don't blame you one bit!" But Christians *are* to blame if we are hateful, short-fused, and impatient. We have no right to foster within ourselves or others a tendency to get even when we have been done a real (or imagined) injustice.

Then others of us excuse our impatience and fieriness with this line: "Well, that's just the way I am, and you'll just have to accept that I'm short-tempered and have to blow off steam." Why should I have to accept that in you? Why should you tolerate it in me? That is the lamest excuse of all for Christians to make, because the central thesis of our religion is that character is changeable when the Spirit of God is present to do his work. That you are "just that way and can't help it" means only that you are trying to hide a defect behind a flimsy excuse, rather than expose it in penitence to the power of God's transforming Spirit.

In the words of J. B. Lightfoot, patience is "self-restraint that does not hastily retaliate a wrong." Or, as I would express it, patience is the discipline of spirit that allows one to bear with people and circumstances until God brings his solution and good purpose to light in the situation. Or, better still:

Patience is the powerful capacity of selfless love to suffer long under adversity. It is that noble ability to bear with either difficult people or adverse circumstances without breaking down. This implies that one has a certain degree of tolerance for the intolerable. It is a generous willingness to try to understand the awkward people or disturbing events that our Father allows to enter our lives.

Over and beyond all of these, patience is that powerful attribute that enables a man or woman to remain steadfast under strain, not just standing still but pressing on. Patience is the potent perseverence that produces positive results even under opposition and suffering. It is love, gracious, self-giving, pressing on, enduring hardship, because of the benefit it may bring to others. It is a quiet willingness to wait, alert and watchful for the right moment to make the appropriate move (W. Phillip Keller. *A Gardener Looks at the Fruits of the Spirit.* Waco, TX: Word Books, 1979, pp. 117, 118).

Surely we want the Spirit of God to build more of this lovely feature of patience into our characters. Yet, the only way he can build it into us is in the context of some sort of adversity. In a situation where we would like to strike back and get even, a divine power is felt to restrain the impulse, turn the other cheek, and return good for evil.

Healing Wounds

Patience is surely designed to be a healing quality in all human relationships.

Impatience is the norm for the sinful nature, so we give harsh word for harsh word, blow for blow, eye for eye, tooth for tooth. We demand too much of one another, of our mates, of our children, of our friends. We sometimes expect the impossible of others and see ourselves as exceptions. We just cannot see that we are not giving as much as we are demanding of other people.

We are sometimes unwilling to let our children grow out of their immature ways, and we expect adult thinking and behavior when they are incapable of either. We can be harsh with employees. We can even feel good about "telling somebody off" or "putting her in her place." We defend our prejudices and justify our condescending behavior toward others. The Spirit of God, when allowed to dwell in us and have his way with us, replaces these ugly traits with patience.

As with all matters holy, Jesus is our perfect example. He waited until he was over thirty years old before beginning his career of public preaching. (Many churches would have been blessed if others of us had lived longer and learned more before unleashing our ministries upon them!) Don't you think he likely had days with those slow, dull-witted disciples, when they were no closer to understanding things of the kingdom after a dozen repetitions than when he first spoke them? Don't you suspect he was provoked to consider retaliation when people said horrible things about him?

Once when Jesus' disciples came in from a preaching tour, John reported contact with a man who was driving out demons in the Nazarene's name. With some degree of apparent satisfaction, he told Jesus, ". . . We tried to stop him, because he is not one of us." Short-tempered John was not about to let some disciple unknown to him go around using the name of Jesus in his ministry. Rather than commend his impatience, the Lord said, "Do not stop him, for whoever is not against you is for you" (Luke 9:49, 50).

But John did not get the message. The very next paragraph of the third Gospel tells how John was in a group of disciples sent ahead of the main party to make preparations for travel along the way to Jerusalem. In a particular Samaritan village on the way, neither the advance party nor Jesus was received hospitably. John and his brother asked, ". . . LORD, do you want us to call down fire from heaven to destroy them?" (Luke 9:54). At that point in his spiritual pilgrimage, John had a short fuse. Jesus rebuked James and John and moved on to another village.

How strange and out of character these two episodes sound to us. You and I know John as the apostle of love. He wasn't always loving. He used to be just as ill-tempered and short with people as some of us are. But the sweet Spirit of God mellowed him to the point that we find it hard to remember him for wanting to call down fire and hinder someone else's ministry. John changed over time. No, that isn't the correct way to say it. John was not the agent of change, but its object. The Spirit of God changed him.

Can you point to specific evidences of spiritual maturity in your life? Perhaps you have noticed yourself becoming a little gentler, mellower, and more tolerant of others than you used to be.

Our impatience with stupidity, laziness, and sin in the lives of others can be our sinful nature asserting itself. Calling somebody else *stupid* implies that we consider ourselves intelligent. Judging her to be lazy says the one passing the judgment is more industrious. Condemning his real or imagined sinfulness may be an attempt to establish one's holiness by contrast. All such condescending arrogance is not in the Spirit of Christ.

Patience Has a Limit

Lest anyone be put on a guilt trip at this point, let me hasten to observe that patience definitely has its limit. *Long*-suffering neither implies nor includes *interminable*-suffering.

Earlier in this chapter, the first part of a verse from the Book of Numbers was cited. The time is right now to return and read the entire verse. "The LORD is slow to anger, abounding in love and forgiving sin and rebellion. *Yet he does not leave the guilty unpunished; he punishes the children for the sin of the fathers to the third and fourth generation"* (14:18, italics added). Being long-fused is not the same as being "forever-fused" with God. At a certain point, he takes no more from his creatures. He leaves them to their own devices, permits them to bring about their own ruin, and judges them for their sins.

There comes a time when you must be like God in that respect. You must have enough character that—after you have been patient, tolerant, and kind—you finally draw the line. Out of respect for God and all that is holy, you must say, "I have reached my limit." Out of respect for your own dignity as a human being, you must declare, "I will take no more."

The temptation is for the sinful nature to give up too quickly and at the first sight of provocation. Life in the Spirit exhibits patience and gives the opportunity for change, repentance, and growth. But even a life in the Spirit must eventually give up. I cannot judge your decision as to when to give up, and you cannot judge mine, for there is no hard-and-fast rule that anybody can lay down in this matter.

At some point, a wife who has been patient and gentle with a rascal is justified in giving up on him. In order to protect herself and save her children, she may have to leave the marriage. Sometimes a child who has been patient with parents has to leave home. And sometimes parents who have been patient with their child have to say through their tears, "We will not and cannot bear more of this. You cannot stay in this house."

Sometimes the church, which is supposed to be the bedrock of patience, gentleness, and love, has to say, "No more." In the same chapter which contains a parable about God's patience with us as the ground for our patience with one another, he gives us a procedure to use when one within the body sins. If a brother sins, go to him, tell him what he has done, and ask him to repent. If he does not, be patient with him and take the next step. Take a couple of people with you, and let them plead. What if he won't hear them? Keep being patient. Get the whole church to assist in the matter. But if he won't hear the whole church, if nobody can get through to him, if he persists in it, if he becomes willful and deliberate and obstinate—withdraw your fellowship from him. We cannot be patient beyond the point at which God can be patient.

Paul required that the church at Corinth excommunicate a certain brother who was guilty of incest and impenitent about his actions (see 1 Cor. 5:1-5). We sometimes have to do the same thing. It isn't that somebody has made us angry, for that is when we are obligated to be tolerant and patient. But when it becomes quite obvious that nothing will change and that the sinful behavior is not due to ignorance or weakness, the line must be drawn. When lying, drunkenness, or marital unfaithfulness is deliberate and persistent, a faithful body of believers must say, "No more."

Reacting to Trials

Because of the experiences Jesus had, we know that our times of stress and trouble elicit his compassion. Whether your challenge is coming from difficult situations or difficult people, he has faced the same sort of grief. "For we have not a high priest who is unable to sympathize with our weaknesses, but we have one who has been tempted in every way just as we are—yet was without sin" (Heb. 4:15).

First, *do not take your trials personally*—as attacks from God. The God we believe in is "the Father of compassion and the God of all comfort" (2 Cor. 1:3b). So when bad things happen and you are tempted to lash out at God, accuse him, or think he has forgotten you, adopt a positive attitude instead. There are no victories without battles. Character develops only as it is tested by the experiences of living. These testing experiences show us our need for God and can drive us closer to him, rather than away from him.

God's grace in a believer's life is not intended to save us from trouble. It is intended to save us from defeat. The storms of disappointment, frustration, and sorrow still come to Christians, but we keep on going, and somehow out of those troubles we find ourselves enriched. After the storms, the beauty of life becomes even more beautiful. So be patient.

Second, *do not confuse Christianity with Stoicism.* It is all right to cry aloud in your pain. It is all right to seek support, encouragement, and comfort from people around you who love you.

In Jesus Christ we see the ultimate divine response to the human predicament. The God who created all things and for whose glory they exist subjected himself to natural laws and human vulnerability. He took the pain of his creation to himself. He became hungry and tired, wept over the death of a friend, knew the agony of being lied about and betrayed, and experienced death.

Third, *praise God—for being your helper in a time of trouble.* Deep, loving relationships are woven from many mundane situations, which do not feel like love at all. When your child is ill, you are by her bedside many hours during the day and night. You are confined to your home, and the stress is intense. Yet you experience an almost overwhelming closeness with the child. You are not concerned about the sleep you are losing but about the child you love. Those are times you treasure—even though she may not remember them or consider them as times of closeness.

God is with us all along, though we may not be aware of his presence. But he is there—keeping watch during long nights of doubt and wrestling. In those times we are surely nearer to God than we can realize. Understanding that life is best measured in nearness to God, instead of the externals of this life, changes the way we look at life in general. Anything which takes you away from God is evil—even if pleasurable, exciting, and done in the context of wealth. Everything which brings you nearer to God—even if unpleasant at the time—is good. "So then, those who suffer according to God's will should commit themselves to their faithful Creator and continue to do good" (1 Peter 4:19).

Fourth, *pray for your way of escape*—and *accept it when God offers it to you.* "God is faithful," wrote Paul; "he will not let you be tempted beyond what you can bear. But when you are tempted, he will also provide a way out so that you can stand up under it" (1 Cor. 10:13). Problems are a part of life. That's just the way the world is, and we can't change or escape that fact. We need to remind ourselves that, tough though they are, there is no problem in the world that cannot be handled—with God's help.

So when your turn comes to drink from the cup of sorrow, draw close to God. Use the power of prayer to unload your soul of its anxieties, knowing that heaven cares. Continue doing what you know is right, trusting the promise of God to keep the person whose heart is fixed on the Lord. Don't be afraid to ask God for the specific things you need, submitting always to his will, and knowing that he will answer according to his wisdom and goodness.

Conclusion

Patience is not learned in times of joy, ease, and leisure. It is built into one's character only through pain. The presence of God's indwelling Spirit gives assurance. His work molds and forms character.

The fruit of the Spirit is *patience.*

7
Kindness

Over a hundred years ago, a woman in a small German town advertised a piano recital she was going to give on a certain day. Her posters falsely identified her as a student of the famous Hungarian composer and pianist Franz Liszt. To her utter dismay, Liszt visited her little village on holiday at the very time of her performance. Knowing she would be found out as a liar and have her budding career ruined by the scandal, she went to the place where Liszt was staying and asked for a conversation with him.

She spoke through tears of embarrassment and humiliation to make her confession to the great man. Liszt responded to her penitence and tears in an unanticipated manner. "You have certainly done a terribly wrong thing," he said, "but we all make mistakes. The only thing to do now is to be sorry, and I think you are truly sorry. Now will you let me hear you play?"

As surprised as she was embarrassed at that point, the girl began to play the piano. She made several errors at first, many of them perhaps caused by her nervousness in the great man's presence. Then, as she gained more confidence, she played better. Liszt corrected her at certain points and made suggestions at key places.

When she had finished, the famous musician said, "My dear, you are now a pupil of Franz Liszt. I have given you instruction this afternoon. Tomorrow you may go on with your concert as advertised. And the last number on the program will be played not by the pupil, but by the teacher."

Can you imagine anyone being that big-hearted? Have you ever had anything like that happen to you? Have you ever done that sort of thing for another person? It was a kindness no one could have deserved from the old man. A man of stature and reputation had had his name misused by a budding, aspiring performer. Having been taken advantage of, he was gracious enough to forgive, save a woman from humiliation, and advance her career.

The King of Kindness

Jesus Christ was the master at that sort of thing. He would reach out to people when there was no reason why he should. He became involved in the lives of people who did not deserve his attention. He befriended the lonely and the unlovely. He built relationships with powerless and unimportant people. By means of his manner, he won the hearts of men and women to God.

Do we imitate Christ in our dealings with people? It is one thing to be indignant and tell someone off who has offended you; it is something else again to be gracious with that person and to win him or her with kindness.

If more of us would learn to live in kindness, the world would be a happier and brighter place for all. Churches would be at peace. Families would be healed. Individual lives could be positive influences in a frequently negative world.

Great souls who are filled with the Spirit of Christ do not look to take offense. They ignore unkindness and refuse to strike back. Because they have been saved through an undeserved kindness which is beyond comprehension, they can treat others graciously.

Kindness is a virtue universally admired. Even people who are not Christians praise this virtue and sometimes even put the followers of Jesus to shame by their deeds. They send relief supplies to Third World countries and disaster sites. Some not only send supplies, but go there personally to administer aid. Following the two devastating earthquakes in Mexico City in 1985, for example, people came from France, Israel, Germany, the United States, and other countries to dig through rubble, at great risk to their own safety, in hope of finding survivors. They left jobs, brought trained dogs and expensive equipment, provided expertise gained in rescuing mountain climbers stranded in snow, and saved lives because of their commitment to being kind.

The special mark which distinguishes *Christian* kindness is its continuation when it is not wanted, appreciated, or returned.

In his Sermon on the Mount, Jesus spoke about loving our enemies, praying for those who persecute us, and otherwise returning good for evil. Notice in particular that he contrasted the tendency of pagans and Gentiles to be kind under some circumstances to the kindness he was calling his followers to display.

> If you love those who love you, what reward will you get? Are not even the tax collectors doing that? And if you greet only your brothers, what are you doing more than others? Do not even pagans do that? Be perfect, therefore, as your heavenly Father is perfect (Matt. 5:46–48).

The natural and expected thing is to be kind to your own, return favor for favor, and scratch the back of the person who scratches yours. But Jesus wants his disciples to do more than that. He wants us to imitate the perfect example of the Father. In the two verses above the lines just quoted, the Father is credited with sending sunshine and rain to both good and evil, righteous and unrighteous. God's routine kindnesses in nature are distributed indiscriminately. Sun and rain, seedtime and harvest, the birth of healthy children, promotions and pay raises—all are distributed among both believers and unbelievers. Every good gift comes from above, no matter who gets it. And that is the model for the way Christians are supposed to distribute their kindnesses.

Of course there are some people who are special in your life. You love your family and do for your own flesh and blood what you cannot do for others. You love your brothers and sisters in Christ and sacrifice to help them through times of special difficulty. And it isn't wrong to receive kindness back from someone to whom you have shown a kindness.

But this quality will be perfected in your life only when you can be generous to those who can never pay you back; kind to people who are likely to accept your kindness without being grateful; and loving to your fellow creatures whom you have reason to expect might somehow use your good deed against you.

The sinful nature demands notice and appreciation which the Spirit can do without. Recently, when my home church was distributing winter coats to some children in our neighborhood, this tension hit me in the face. I delivered three coats to a lady for her eight-, ten-, and fourteen-year-old children. She accepted them, blew cigarette smoke in my direction, and flicked cigarette ashes at my feet. She uttered not one word of gratitude. As I turned to leave her house, I was thinking, "Would it have been too much for her to offer a 'thank you' for a hundred dollars' worth of clothing?" God forgive me! I had lost sight of why we were clothing children in the first place. It wasn't for our neighbors' appreciation, but for God's glory that we were doing it. The flesh has been crucified with Christ, but it squirms to get down off the cross!

The spring of kindness is honest concern about other people, and the guideline for showing kindness is respect for other people. You are not being kind, no matter how generous your deed is, if you are condescending and haughty in performing it. You are not being kind if you put the person down and denigrate his worth by saying, in essence, "I'm doing for you what you should have been able to do for yourself."

And kindness will always involve risk. Somebody won't appreciate what you do. Someone else might even turn on you or take your kindness as a symbol of weakness. People have been manipulated in their attempts to show kindness by what might be called "guilt-gotchas." A guilt-gotcha is when someone comes at you with: "If you were really a Christian, you would do so-and-so for me"; or "If you really wanted to be kind, you would do this." In spite of the risks, Christians keep on showing kindness. This is what distinguishes humanitarianism from kindness as an element of the fruit of the Spirit.

One of the best efforts at characterizing kindness has been made by Lewis Smedes. He calls kindness:

> . . . the power to move *close* to another person in order to heal. The pity that wells up in us after watching a television documentary about starving children is not kindness. Kindness is the strength to take the starving child in your arms and feed it at your own breast. Kindness is the power to heal a leper by washing his wounds

with your own hands. Kindness is the power to bear another's burdens by feeling his pain in your own soul (Lewis B. Smedes. *Love Within Limits*. Grand Rapids: William B. Eerdmans Publishing Company, 1978, p. 16).

Put most simply, kindness is one's willingness to become involved in another's need.

We Resist Kindness

Our sinful nature causes us to draw back from the risks inherent with becoming involved in others' needs.

It was almost two decades ago that the story of Kitty Genovese was carried in the newspapers. Miss Genovese was murdered on a New York City street as thirty-eight persons ignored her repeated screams. Her attacker came and left several times, while neighbors pulled down their windows to avoid hearing her screams. They refused to get involved. They didn't even call the police.

More recently, the Associated Press carried the story of a dozen people who watched and did nothing as three youths with a shotgun robbed a pleading man in Saint Louis. A 56-year-old man said he was leaving a restaurant about 10:45 P.M. when three teenagers took his money and car. "Nobody helped," he said. "There were at least a dozen people there, and nobody tried to stop it or call the police."

Just one night before in the same city, three youths kicked and beat a female bus driver outside Busch Memorial Stadium, as hundreds of fans leaving the sports arena ignored her screams. "There was a whole crowd of people out on that ramp, and I kept pleading for help," she told the reporter, "but nobody stopped. Nobody offered to help."

We're afraid. We don't want to get involved. We don't want to be at risk. While discretion may be the better part of valor in certain situations, we could at least go for help or call the police.

In the same summer these two disheartening incidents in Saint Louis took place, there was another episode in that city which contrasted sharply. It also made national news. It was the story of an eleven-year-old boy named Sur Williams. He rode his bicycle to get the police after seeing a girl being raped in a park—while more than twenty adult onlookers did nothing. Suddenly Sur was a hero. Everyone wanted him to explain his bravery. His humble answer was this: "I was just doing what my mother told me to do."

I suspect all of us were taught by our mothers, fathers, Sunday-school teachers, and personal consciences that we have an obligation to other people in our world. Maybe Sur Williams's action prompted some of us to recall what we were suppressing and to begin listening to our hearts again.

For the beautiful virtue of kindness, we are prone to substitute things like speeches and chapters in books. Or perhaps we substitute tears. Most generally in our society, we set up an agency. Then we send hungry and homeless people to the office of that agency.

Government agencies may turn out to be a death blow to Christian kindness. They may be the very damnation of a lot of us church folk. For although it is right for those agencies to exist and offer their services, it is not right for us to let them take over the front lines in the battle against sickness, poverty, and the like. That is where the church belongs.

The primary medical clinic for the poor in my neighborhood should be the one we believers have put in place. The place where hungry people can be fed should be staffed by Christians, rather than non-Christian humanitarians. The place where people whose families are hurting can go for help should be the neighborhood assembly of saints. The place where people can go to find somebody who cares and who will put their arms around them must be wherever one of us who wears the name of Christ is.

Kindness ought to be the hallmark of the people of God. We should be known in our communities as ministers to the needs of people. But look what we have done with the word *minister*. We use it to refer to that small percentage of any church's membership who are paid professionals on the congregation's staff. Always careful to spell the word with a capital letter *M*, we identify the Minister of Education, the Minister to Youth, the Minister of Evangelism, and so on. But the word translated *minister* in the New Testament actually means servant or slave, and ministry is the role of every believer. We are to be God's servants and voluntary slaves to one another in love.

Christians ought to be known as people of kind hearts, kind words, and kind deeds. Whether we are educating children, tending to the sick, building hospitals, teaching English to newcomers in our culture, or sharing the gospel with someone, it is kindness in action.

The Kindness of God

Since the goal identified for us by Jesus in the Sermon on the Mount is imitation of God's indiscriminate kindness, perhaps it will help us to look at a few verses from Scripture about God's exhibition of this virtue.

Look first at the language of Ephesians 2:6, 7: "God raised us up with Christ and seated us with him in the heavenly realms in Christ Jesus, in order that in the coming ages he might show the incomparable riches of his grace, expressed in his kindness to us in Christ Jesus."

Notice how the words *grace* and *kindness* are linked in this text. Kind deeds are always acts of grace. They are undeserved and performed without calculation of what is to be expected in return. As Paul observed, the greatest exhibit of God's kindness to us is in the person of Christ Jesus.

Look next at Titus 3:4, 5. The language is startlingly similar to that of the verse just noted. "But when the kindness and love of God our Savior appeared, he saved us, not because of righteous things we had done, but because of his mercy."

There you have it. A triad of beautiful traits in the essential nature of our God: *kindness, love,* and *mercy.* The righteous things you and I may (or may *not*) do have nothing to do with God's nature. His willingness to save us through the Son is predicated on his kindness rather than our worth.

Look again at Romans 11:22. Here is a verse that calls us to realize that God's kindness is more than sentimentality. There is a certain toughness to the kind nature of our God. The passage says: "Consider therefore the kindness and sternness of God: sternness to those who fell, but kindness to you, provided that you continue in his kindness."

If you will accept the love and grace of God, his essential kindness is ever before you. Because of his mercifully kind attitude toward his sinful creatures, he does not give up on even one who desires him. Yet if a proud and arrogant man deliberately rejects divine mercy or tries to manipulate God's love, he will not get by with it. God's kindness is not tepid indifference to evil. God can be stern. He has enough character to draw the line beyond which he will not tolerate evil.

The Kindness of God's People

Because God is kind, his people can also be kind. His nature can be reproduced in ours. Bearing the fruit of the Spirit is a process whereby the old, sinful nature is replaced with the character traits which belong to a Holy God.

Because the Spirit of God indwells us, the sinful tendency to be unfeeling and uncaring begins to be overcome by the power of love. The old inclination to remain uninvolved, and to keep things that might cause us discomfort at arm's length, is replaced by a willingness to be at risk for the sake of others. We are able to sacrifice of ourselves for them. We begin to see healing occur in lives where God's kindness has reached to hurting and lost people through his children.

One of the specific cases where kindness is always appropriate (but frequently lacking) has to do with the judgments we make about one another. Jesus spoke to this issue in the Sermon on the Mount:

> Do not judge, or you too will be judged. For the same way you judge others, you will be judged and with the measure you use, it will be measured to you.
>
> Why do you look at the speck of sawdust in your brother's eye and pay no attention to the plank in your own eye? How can you say to your brother 'Let me take the speck out of your eye,' when all the time there is a plank in your own eye? (Matt. 7:1-4).

It would be hard to miss the humor of Jesus' censure against the common human tendency to sit in judgment on one another with harshness, as opposed to generosity and kindness. A man with a wooden beam in his eye is offering to pick a tiny splinter or speck of sawdust out of another's eye. Absurd? Typical. A

man picks at the sins of others, while refusing to face up to
the glaring failures of his own life. Unthinkable? Commonplace.
The command "Do not judge" is certainly not absolute. We
cannot avoid making judgments. We make ethical judgments
about lying and breaking faith. We make distinctions between
truth and error. But sometimes we tend to become professional
critics and begin to specialize in shoot-from-the-hip condemnation. It is this pitfall that Jesus was warning against in his
statement about capricious judgment. Kindness of spirit is the
best safeguard against such a disposition.

Some religionists of Jesus' day had cultivated a critical spirit
toward their brothers and were anything but kind in the way
they treated one another. They carped at people who failed to
tithe tiny little herbs in their gardens and pronounced ringing
anathemas against those who differed with them on the
interpretation of the law of Moses. In their daily lives, however,
those same people were neglecting the weightier matters of
justice, mercy, and faith. The anger of Jesus toward such behavior
is apparent more than once in the Gospels.

Perhaps the most frightening thing about Jesus' teaching on
the matter of judging others is this: each of us will be judged
by the same standard of charity (or lack thereof) we show others.
Sharp-tongued criticism and unkind judgments are spiritual
boomerangs. They always come back and hit us flush in the face.

It really does work that way, doesn't it? The person who is
always criticizing and finding fault invites other people to watch
him like a hawk. His own sins—and none is without sin—will
then be judged severely when they come to light. On the other
hand, the person who is kind and gracious toward others receives
similar treatment in his own dark hour of the soul. Presumably,
there will be this same sort of judgment in kind at the last day.

When you see or hear something which could discredit another
if given a certain interpretation, look for a way to interpret it
positively. Think the best of others, and they will think better
of you.

If you see someone do something positively evil, or if he sins
against you personally, be eager to forgive and do all you can
to minimize the harm which the deed could bring to him. Be
slow to expose and eager to show kindness, and others will deal

more kindly with your own foibles and failures. Just as censure breeds censure, kindness generates kindness.

Pursuing the theme that final judgment will reflect the degree of kindness one has shown to others, Jesus made the same point in Matthew 25. His point is not to say that our salvation is earned by the kind deeds we do, but that kind deeds will be reflected in the life experiences of someone who is saved.

In a preview of that day, Jesus envisions himself acknowledging kind deeds done to him by those on his right hand. He was hungry, and they fed him; he was thirsty, and they gave him something to drink; he was in prison, and they visited him. Confused by his words because many of them did not even live on earth during the time Jesus tabernacled in flesh, they ask: "When did we see you sick or in prison and go to visit you?" (see v. 37).

Jesus' answer rebukes all those who think the work of the church is done only in assemblies and in public view and exalts all whose behind-the-scenes activity nobody knows. "The King will reply, 'I tell you the truth, whatever you did for one of the least of these brothers of mine, you did for me'" (Matt. 25:40).

Kind people don't have to have spotlights to be about their special ministries. There are seldom cameras around when the poor are being fed by Christians. There are never large crowds to cheer when you sacrifice time to visit someone in prison. When you become involved with helping an alcoholic, there will be more raised eyebrows than anything else.

Commenting on acts of kindness which some would show his disciples, Jesus once said, "And if anyone gives even a cup of cold water to one of these . . . he will certainly not lose his reward" (v. 42).

Christians are to be clothed with kindness (Col. 3:12). Or, as Paul expressed it elsewhere, "Be kind and compassionate to one another, forgiving each other, just as in Christ God forgave you" (Eph. 4:32).

Before leaving this matter of kindness in Christian character, it should be stressed that kindness doesn't equate with being naive and wimpy. Just as the kindness of God can exhibit toughness when appropriate, so must ours. God says *no* to some of the things we try to get by with, but remains kind, nevertheless. A parent sometimes has to draw the line with his or her child.

Individual believers and entire churches sometimes have to say *no* also.

Kindness is not sweeping things under the carpet. It is not spineless tolerance toward evil. It can never be prostituted into the indulgence of that which is wrong.

Kindness is not the withholding of truth, but telling the truth with compassion for the person confronted by it. It is not holding back from rebuke when rebuke is called for, but administering the rebuke lovingly and forgiving easily.

To be concerned without being condescending, to be merciful without being manipulative, to be helpful without being haughty—these are godly expressions of kindness. To learn to live this way is to rise above the level of your sinful nature and to demonstrate the presence of the Spirit of God in your life.

Conclusion

The natural process is to be kind to people who are being kind to you and to ignore or abuse those who are ignoring or mistreating you. The general rule of human conduct seems to be that you can afford to show kindness if there is good reason to think that doing so will bring a positive return. Pagans love *that* way!

The *unnatural* way of conduct is to love as God loves. Give without expecting to get anything back. Be charitable without selfish motives. Show kindness without waiting to find out if it is appreciated. This is the way God loves. Just as sunshine and rain and good gifts are given to all people by a kind God, his child develops a lifestyle that exudes kindness to everybody.

Norman Cousins is an insightful thinker and writer. He makes no claim to being a Christian. He is a humanist. Because of his perspective as an "outsider" to Christianity, some of his observations about us may be all the more significant. Someone looking at us from the outside can sometimes see us more clearly than we can see ourselves. He says:

> Never before have there been so many churches and temples; never before has the institution of man been in greater jeopardy. Christianity has not truly involved itself in the human situation. It has become strangely adjacent to the crisis of man, seemingly

content with trying to create a moral and spiritual atmosphere instead of becoming a towering and dominant force in the shaping of a world congenial to man. It has become one of the values we fight for instead of a force in itself. It is not regarded as the working source of wisdom and strength for conscience. It has yet to become supremely pertinent and supremely effective in safeguarding the commonwealth of man at a time of peril so profound as to be incomprehensible to the rational intelligence alone (Norman Cousins. *Human Options.* New York: W. W. Norton & Company, 1981, p. 43).

If I understand what he is saying to us, he is chiding us for turning the church into an institution which exists for itself. He sees no value to a church which congratulates itself for a defensive posture and applauds itself for being aloof, when the cry of a hurting world is to have someone in its midst to touch it and care for it and heal its wounds. Jesus did precisely that. Too often, however, his church does not.

Kindness is one's willingness to become involved in the needs of another. It is the virtue which is lacking when we avoid the hurts of this world and insulate ourselves from its pain.

The fruit of the Spirit is *kindness*.

8

Goodness

Goodness (Gk, *agathōsynē*) is probably the most difficult of the nine traits identified as the fruit of the Spirit to define adequately. In English and Greek, the term finds its meaning from the deed or quality which exhibits it. The word is sometimes vague as to its content.

A variety of meanings can be attached to the adjective *good* in English. I may tell you about the good watch that my good wife gave me for my birthday several years ago. You may describe for me a good course you are taking at the university or the good job you look forward to every day. Or you may tell me about your good friend who did a good deed for you yesterday. The word can be used to describe very different entities.

At its lowest common denominator, the adjectival form of the word probably means something like "serviceable, useful for a specific purpose." Thus, a good watch is one that keeps time accurately, a good course covers its subject matter in a helpful way, a good deed meets a need in someone's life, and so forth.

Jesus reflected the varied use of the Greek term meaning good in his vocabulary. In Matthew 7:17 he refers to the fact that "every good tree bears good fruit." In his Parable of the Soils, he speaks of some seed falling into "good soil" (Luke 8:8). Good fruit trees are the ones which serve their purpose of yielding edible fruit, good fruit meets the body's need for nourishment, and good soil is useful for growing crops.

From its biblical and nonbiblical usage, the total word group we are examining here (that is, goodness, good, doing good) appears to involve a dual element when used as a theological concept. Here is a definition that seems to me to fit the word and then attempt to justify it by examining some passages from the Word of God: *Goodness is that which is both upright and honorable as combined with and tempered by generosity.*

We would expect to find the notion of uprightness in any theological uses of the words which relate to *goodness.* Because of God's holiness, any virtue or activity which honors him or serves his purpose would certainly have to be honorable and upright. The latter idea of generosity might not suggest itself as easily and directly. After all, we sometimes connect uprightness with sternness and actions which are honorable with an absolute refusal to make allowances for anyone's shortcomings in relation to them.

It is easy enough to show that this proffered definition fits a number of the word's appearances in Scripture. For example, one might examine such verses as Mark 10:17, 18, Romans 8:28, and Ephesians 2:10 to see that such a definition does no injustice to scriptural statements about the nature of God, his workings on behalf of his people, and the things he would like to see in our lives. Because God is both upright and generous, he always acts accordingly in the affairs of his people. So, it follows as a matter of course that he would wish for us to be both upright and generous in what we do.

But it is one thing to offer a definition for a term—and then show that such an understanding will fit selected texts—and something else to justify such a definition from hard data. It is to this task that we must give attention before proceeding further.

Justifying a Definition of "Goodness"

How can one hope to show that goodness, when considered as a spiritual virtue in the Bible, entails the dual concept of uprightness and charity? How might one justify combining behavior which is honorable with actions exhibiting generosity in one and the same word?

We begin with the obvious truth that the antithesis to good is, of course, evil. Goodness and wickedness are polar opposites. God is the personal embodiment of goodness; Satan is the epitome of evil. This antithesis works itself out throughout the Word of God. In each of the three texts about to be examined, focus particularly on the word which is always the opposite of good. Watch how the word *evil* consistently involves a miserly spirit, as well as some dastardly deed. Since this is the case, its spiritual opposite must, of necessity, involve not only an honorable action, but a generous spirit to accompany it.

First, look to one of the Psalms of the Old Testament. The background of this Davidic Psalm takes us to 1 Samuel 8:21, 22. When Israel chose her first king, the nation chose the wrong man at the wrong time for the wrong reasons. The fatal flaw in his character, which would have prohibited God from choosing him for the role in the first place, had shown itself in his arrogant behavior and disobedience. He would not be allowed to remain as king. God made known his intention to replace the man after Israel's heart with the man after his own heart. Samuel had anointed David to the throne. Wicked and jealous man that he was, Saul set about to murder David because of the threat he represented to his position in the nation.

In the course of David's flight from Saul, he reached Nob and presented himself to Ahimelech the priest. The latter provided David with some provisions and a weapon. (The weapon, ironically, was the sword of Goliath, which David had taken earlier from the giant Philistine when he killed him.)

An agent of Saul learned of David's visit to Nob and that the priest had assisted him with food and a sword. One day when King Saul was throwing a tantrum before his men about his jeopardy and complaining that no one was doing anything to help him, that servant saw his opportunity for self-advancement in the king's eyes. He stepped forward and volunteered what he knew about David and Ahimelech. Saul rushed to Nob and searched for David. Not finding him, he turned on Ahimelech and the other members of his priestly family. He ordered his men to kill them. When they showed more piety than their king by refusing to murder God's priests, Saul turned to the servant who had started this entire sordid affair by telling of David's visit to Nob and ordered him to do the murderous deed.

The man massacred an entire town, killing men, women, children, and animals.

The man whose treacherous tongue led to an atrocity at Nob was named Doeg the Edomite. Psalm 52 is written about him.

> Why do you boast of evil, you mighty man?
>   Why do you boast all day long,
>   you who are a disgrace in the eyes of God?
> Your tongue plots destruction;
>   it is like a sharpened razor,
>   you who practice deceit.
> You love evil rather than good,
>   falsehood rather than speaking the truth.
> You love every harmful word,
>   O you deceitful tongue! (Ps. 52:1–4).

Doeg advanced his career, at least temporarily, by dishonorable and self-seeking conduct. By treachery and using his tongue against God's anointed king and priests, he ingratiated himself to King Saul. He advanced his personal interests by betraying innocent people who had done nothing but give brief and temporary assistance to the man on whom God's favor rested. In so doing, he aligned himself with the rebellious and wicked Saul.

Thus, David said of him, "He loved evil rather than good" (see v. 3). That he loved evil was proved by his treachery and deceit. He did a dishonorable thing from a perverse and self-seeking motive. He had no defense of ignorance to offer. It was not that he had acted with the intention of honoring God or showing mercy to innocent people. Although he was by occupation a shepherd rather than a soldier, he was able to give his hand to the slaughter of innocent people when hardened military men who had taken life before hesitated. His heart had no mercy, charity, or love. Therefore, no deed, regardless of how wicked, was beneath him.

Remember, please, that Doeg did not tell a lie. All he told Saul was true. David really had been at Nob, contacted Ahimelech, and accepted items from the priest. So what made Doeg's behavior evil was not that he falsified the facts of the case, but that he used truth treacherously and with a purely selfish motive. Without regard to God, God's anointed, or innocent people, he acted to advance himself before Saul.

What is goodness? It is honorable and upright conduct tempered by generosity. Whatever else Doeg was, he was not a good man—even when he was relating the truth.

Second, notice a contrast between *good* and *evil* in the teaching of Jesus. It is found in the context of some instruction he gave his disciples about the relative worth of heavenly treasure versus earthly mammon.

> The eye is the lamp of the body. If your eyes are good, your whole body will be full of light. But if your eyes are bad [evil, KJV], your whole body will be full of darkness. If then the light within you is darkness, how great is that darkness (Matt. 6:22, 23).

This text used to puzzle me. What does eyesight have to do with anything spiritual? How do the eyes relate to one's right or wrong use of wealth? The interpretation of the passage becomes evident when you realize that "eyes" here are to be understood not of one's physical organs of sight but of his perspective on and attitude toward wealth.

Someone with a "good eye" sees positive uses for wealth, gains whatever amount of money and property he attains by honorable means, and is generous with the prosperity God has given him. On the other hand, someone with an "evil eye" sees selfish and/or wicked possibilities money can realize, pursues it by any means possible, and is miserly and mean with what comes to him.

Third, see how Jesus uses the terms *good* and *evil* in the Parable of the Workers in the Vineyard. Here, too, he contrasts the two terms and thereby gives us insight into what goodness is.

The story begins with a man hiring workers at daybreak one morning to work in his vineyard. He contracts with them at the rate of one denarius per day—a typical wage for field workers at the time. Three hours later, he hires still more workers. He does the same thing again at noon and at midafternoon. Finally, with only one hour of daylight left, he hires a final group of workers to go into his fields. When the sun goes down, he pays every single worker a denarius. At that, some of the people who had worked longer and in the heat of the day complained. They accused the owner of the vineyard of being unfair.

But he answered one of them, "Friend, I am not being unfair to you. Didn't you agree to work for a denarius? Take your pay and go. I want to give the man who was hired last the same as I gave you. Don't I have the right to do what I want with my own money? Or are you envious because I am generous?" (Matt. 20:13–15).

The last line of this quotation literally reads: "Is your eye evil because I am good?" The problem in the parable was with some who had an evil (that is, miserly, envious) perspective on a good (that is, generous, charitable) deed.

In ancient times it was taken for granted that every man had the right to do with his property whatever he chose to do with it. It was his and could be held, sold, or given away at his discretion. So the master in the story defended himself against the charge that he had acted dishonorably by being generous to the latecomers. He reminded the complainers that he was fulfilling his contract with them. He offered to pay them a denarius for the day's work, and they accepted the offer. He acted honorably and did just as he said he would. What he was being criticized for was not a failure to meet his obligation to the first workers, but his surprising liberality with the last ones.

If you are still having problems with the story as it stands because of our modern notions of management and labor, perhaps it helps to realize that the parable was designed to defend God against the charge that he was being unjust and dishonorable by accepting outcasts and Gentiles into the kingdom of heaven.

The Jews had been God's chosen people for ages. Some of them were being extremely critical of Jesus because he was eating with tax collectors and sinners, and even pointing to a time when pagans would be accepted into the kingdom. The parable was directed at their criticisms. It was designed to communicate this message: Salvation is heaven's free gift. No one earns it by his labors for God—whether many or few. He offers it freely to all who will enter his vineyard. If the Jews have had access to special covenants and promises for a longer time, they have no right to feel offended that God now offers the Gentiles equal access. God is neither unfair nor dishonorable. He is simply more generous than some can understand or tolerate. Anyone with such an attitude is looking at God's actions through an "evil eye," being miserly with divine grace, and acting like an envious child who wants another's birthday presents.

Goodness consists of acting honorably and fairly with all, yet tempering that honesty and integrity with generosity. And that is why goodness offends evil people. Goodness insults wicked people, for they look at all things selfishly and begrudge anyone else good fortune.

Understanding the Trait

One of the best ways to understand goodness as a virtue in human behavior is with a case study in the Book of Acts. Luke says of the man Barnabas, "He was a good man, full of the Holy Spirit . . ." (Acts 11:24). It is of no small interest to me that the goodness of the man is mentioned in immediate proximity to an affirmation that he was filled with the Spirit of God! What traits in the life of this man allowed the sacred writer to call him a *good* man?

The first time we meet him in the Lucan record of the early church, he was acting with special generosity toward his needy brothers in Christ (4:36, 37). Once, when some poor members of the Jerusalem church needed assistance, Barnabas sold a piece of land he owned. He then proceeded to give the total income from it into the treasury of the church.

The next time we see him in the record, he is using his personal credibility among the believers to help a new convert be accepted into the body (9:26-29). When Paul came to Jerusalem after his conversion, some of the brothers were reluctant to receive him because they knew his track record as a persecutor. They could not bring themselves to believe that he had really changed so completely. It was Barnabas who put his arm around him, introduced him to the church, and vouched for the genuineness of his faith. On the basis of an immense credibility, based on demonstrated integrity within the group, Barnabas secured Paul's reception into the fellowship of that church.

A couple of chapters later, Luke tells how the disciples in Jerusalem learned that a church had been established among the Gentiles up in Antioch of Syria (11:22-26). The apostles decided to select somebody who could go there with their blessing to stabilize it. And whom did they choose? It was Barnabas. He was the kind of man who would make any church stable and better by his presence.

Then, when the church at Antioch decided that the word they had received must go forth into the whole world, they prayed for God to show them who to send on the grand missionary enterprise they envisioned. The Holy Spirit led them to set apart Barnabas and Paul for the work (13:1–3).

The "good man" Barnabas was generous on behalf of needy people. He had credibility among the disciples because of his personal character. He was the sort of man whose personality and work would make a church stronger. He was evangelistic in outlook. These qualities do not stand independently of the fact that he was a good man. They identify the specific ways his goodness demonstrated itself.

We sometimes let "She's a good woman" or "He's a fine man" trip off our tongues too easily. To be a genuinely good person is to be somebody whose character is of the same bolt of fabric as the man Barnabas. Goodness is a part of the fruit of the Spirit and was an evident part of his character precisely because he was filled with the Spirit. Even the worst of men can do occasional good deeds, but goodness as a discernible and dominant theme in a life comes from being filled with the same Spirit who lived in Barnabas. It was God who made him good, not Barnabas himself.

Displaying the Virtue

No one is good who does not exhibit uprightness, honesty, and integrity. Yet, it would be possible to imagine someone who was scrupulous in this respect, but was harsh and hateful with people who fell short of his standards. So, the biblical virtue of goodness includes not only these virtues but compassion and generosity as well.

A good person is honorable in conduct without being condescending toward those who act dishonorably; righteous without being self-righteous; urgent to defend the truth without leaving the impression that he knows all of it himself; and separated from sin without setting himself up as the judge of others' behavior.

In the corporate life of the church, we must be upright people who love God, live truth, and walk humbly. While never abandoning holiness, we must still be willing to reach out and touch others struggling beside us on the path of life. We must practice a sense of genuine community that allows the world to see our love for one another as we exhibit Christ's holiness to the world.

The late Francis Schaeffer expressed it this way:

> The heart of these sets of principles is to show forth the love of God and the holiness of God *simultaneously.* If we show either of these without the other, we exhibit not the character, but a caricature of God for the world to see. If we stress the love of God without the holiness of God, it turns out only to be compromise. But if we stress the holiness of God without the love of God, we practice something that is hard and lacks beauty. And it is important to show forth beauty before a lost world and a lost generation. All too often young people have not been wrong in saying that the church is ugly. In the name of our Lord Jesus Christ we are called upon to show to a watching world and to our own young people that the church is something beautiful.
>
> Several years ago I wrestled with the question of what was wrong with much of the church that stood for purity. I came to the conclusion that in the flesh we can stress purity without love or we can stress the love of God without purity, but that in the flesh we cannot stress both simultaneously. In order to exhibit both simultaneously, we must look moment by moment to the work of Christ, to the work of the Holy Spirit (Francis A. Schaeffer. *The Church Before the Watching World.* Downers Grove, IL: Inter-Varsity Press, 1971, p. 63).

He is right. The tension in the lives of struggling believers comes from trying to do spiritual things in the power of the flesh. Sometimes we try to be loving and fail to uphold the holiness of God and rightness of the gospel demand of repentance. Sometimes we try to uphold purity and come across as being so abrasive and judgmental. It is only in "surrenderedness" to the Spirit of God that we can keep the two in proper balance and exhibit the holiness and the love of God simultaneously.

As the fruit of the Spirit, it is goodness that produces upright conduct, tempered by the generosity which makes righteousness appealing to those who see it.

When I was in junior high school, a lady wanted to give me some of her tropical fish. I was thrilled at the idea because they were beautiful. I told my mother about it, and she was willing. But we had to find an aquarium to keep them in. As we started searching for a glass container to convert into an aquarium, we found something that we thought was perfect. It was a glass cylinder from an old gasoline pump. Although it was long before the time of most who will read this book, gasoline pumps used to have large glass containers at the top where you would pump several gallons of gasoline and then drain the fuel into your car. Well, we found one of those old pumps in a junkyard with its glass still unbroken. We got permission from the owner to remove the glass and were very careful with it.

Only when we got it home did we realize how dirty the tank was. But we scrubbed and cleaned for hours. Then we put in colored gravel, plants, lights, and an aerator. We claimed our tropical fish from the lady who had offered them. It was beautiful! That dirty, ugly glass tank had become the home for seven beautiful and delicate creatures.

The next morning, however, two of them were floating belly-up. By the end of the day, there were two or three more dead. And by the following morning, not one was still alive. We knew we had done something wrong but had no idea what. We went back to the lady who had given them to me and told her with embarrassment what had become of the fish. I explained all the trouble we had gone to with the tank to fix it up as an aquarium. Pretty soon she interrupted and said she knew what the trouble was. We had washed the tank with soap, and that is an absolute no-no when dealing with delicate little tropical fish. Our uninformed efforts at trying to make something beautiful had destroyed the lives we were trying to protect.

Sometimes we do a very similar thing in the church. In our zeal to clean up our lives and those of others, we use caustic cleansers—harsh criticism, condemnation, outbursts of temper. We think we are doing right and defending holiness, but our harsh treatment is more than some fragile souls can bear. So some in the church, especially some who are still very young in years as well as faith, die. And people on the outside who see all the dead bodies we float to the surface want nothing to do with the church. They don't want to subject themselves to the same caustic process which they have seen kill others.

We must plead for and allow the Spirit of God to build goodness into our hearts and churches. We will know he is present when we have learned to protect the integrity and purity of the Word of God with mercy and love.

In our evangelistic outreach, love must be allowed to temper
our manner without compromising the gospel we preach. We
must never shrink from lifting up Christ, proclaiming the gospel,
and defending the faith. But we must do so without a trace of
smugness and without giving the impression that we are pleased
that sinners without him are lost.

A while back I was reading of a man who was led to Christ
by a gentle soul named T. B. Larimore. The man in question
had been to hundreds of church services and dozens of
evangelistic meetings before Larimore came and preached in the
town. So someone asked him, "Why did you respond to the gospel
under Brother Larimore's preaching when you hadn't before?" His
answer is a rebuke to some of us and our methods. "From other
preachers I'd learned I was going to hell," he said, "but they seemed
pleased that I was. From Larimore I learned I was going to hell,
but I could tell it broke his heart to have to tell me so."

The Bible tells us to be prepared always to explain and defend
our faith in Jesus. But Scripture says to make that presentation
"with gentleness and respect, keeping a clear conscience" (1 Peter
3:15b, 16a). Let us preach the gospel with such gentleness and
respect that we can have a clear conscience about it. And there
is no way to have a clear conscience in upholding the holiness
of God and the truth of his word if we end up slaying the sinner
in the process.

The sinner is not my enemy. The sinner is in the clutches
of my enemy, and I must not destroy the sinner while trying
to free him from Satan. Otherwise I accomplish Satan's end by
my foolish, fumbling attempts with the truth. The Word of God
is the sword of the Spirit (Eph. 6:17), and I must use the sword
to cut the cords of sin which hold the sinner—and not to lop
his head off.

When we serve others in Jesus' name with good works, we need
to do it with the goodness which is appropriate to such service.

Remember Dorcas? The text says of her in Acts 9:36 that
she was a woman "full of good works" (KJV) or "who was always
doing good" (NIV). At her death there were people left to mourn
her who had been blessed by her gracious life. She had made
clothing for them with her own hands. She had doubtless helped
them in other ways as well.

She must have been the sort of person in whom no one

suspected a hidden agenda. One who does right, lives by lofty principles, and exhibits integrity will be judged trustworthy by others. Then that person can minister without being suspect and serve without being feared for a possible ulterior motive.

Recently, one of our daily papers in Nashville carried the story of a woman who was involved in taking care of a little three-year-old, sexually abused child in a local hospital. She is a volunteer whom the nursing staff called in right after the little girl was admitted and had to have surgery. The woman stayed at the hospital continuously for the first twenty-four hours. At first the little girl would not even look at her, but she just stayed with her and rocked her and sang to her softly. About halfway through that first day, the frightened little girl began to make eye contact with her. After a while she began to cry and squeeze the woman's neck. By the end of that day, the hurt child was beginning to heal emotionally as well as physically. Someone—one who cared about her from a pure heart, was willing to give of herself without making demands, and was gentle in every word and deed—won the confidence of a child who had been a victim of such a horrible trauma that it might have made it impossible for her ever to trust another human being.

When we minister in Jesus' name, it would be helpful to remember that woman's approach as a model. Some people are so hurt by life that they cannot hold their heads up and look us in the eye. They are embarrassed to have to ask for food or clothing for their children. They are humiliated by their personal sins. Our role is simply to stay with them, serve them, love them—and allow God to begin to heal them.

Conclusion

Spirit-prompted goodness and the resulting good character, good name, and good works in a believer's life are totally different from the good works someone might attempt for the sake of merit before God. The former lifestyle of divine goodness being formed within us and exhibited in our actions is the fruit of the Spirit; the latter is a pious fraud perpetrated for the selfish purpose of seeking attention or praise.

A biblical case in point would be Barnabas's good act of generosity contrasted with Ananias's and Sapphira's mock act of generosity. What Barnabas did originated with a noble motive, but what Ananias and Sapphira did was prompted from the desire to be noticed for their piety.

A rule of thumb for separating Spirit-generated goodness from its counterfeit is this: How do you react when your goodness is misunderstood, rejected, taken advantage of, or turned back on you? If anger and thoughts of retaliation rise up, that probably indicates you were acting out of an impure motive to start with. If forgiveness and returning good for evil are involved in your response, that demonstrates the presence of the Spirit of God in your life and exhibits genuine goodness.

Unfortunately, a good person will occasionally suffer episodes of being victimized. He will polarize people by his goodness. Jesus did. His goodness attracted some people to him and repelled the ones who were pious frauds. Yet he did not call down fire and brimstone. He did not invoke divine wrath. Jesus turned the other cheek and went like a lamb to the slaughter. He offered salvation to the very people who had rejected him. That was goodness arising from the Spirit of God in him.

The fruit of the Spirit is *goodness.*

9
Faithfulness

The words *faith* and *faithfulness* are closely related. One's faith in another is based on that person's demonstrated faithfulness. Faithfulness is the quality that makes a person utterly reliable, utterly loyal, utterly dependable—in word and deed.

A better word than *faithfulness* to translate the Greek term *pistis* would probably be our English term *dependability*. It is an indicator of the Spirit's presence in a believer to watch for consistent, long-term dependability in that person's life.

Remember in the Parable of the Soils that Jesus spoke of seed falling on rocky soil? The seed which fell into that shallow layer of earth covering solid rock sprang up quickly, but then died because of a lack of nourishment. "Those on the rock are the ones who receive the word with joy when they hear it, but they have no root. They believe for a while, but in the time of testing they fall away" (Luke 8:13). The people represented in this figure are those who lack dependability, faithfulness, reliability. They may begin well, but simply cannot last over the long haul. They lack the depth necessary to make them dependable.

God Is Faithful

Over and over the Bible affirms that one of the primary attributes for which God is to be praised is his faithfulness. God

123

is always dependable. He makes his word good. He always acts consistently with both holiness and love.

It is interesting to note how the Bible links stability in the lives of Christians to divine faithfulness. Thus, one finds statements like: "Let us hold unswervingly to the hope we profess, for he who promised is faithful" (Heb. 10:23). The reason a Christian is able to stand when life's howling storms come against him is that his faith is grounded in a God whose promises to him will always be honored.

Following the statement just quoted about God's faithfulness comes the famous Hebrews 11 with its enumeration of people who lived by faith. By trusting that God's promises to them were reliable, they gained victories over various ordeals and trials.

Abraham, Israel's "Father of the Faithful," is praised with these words: "By faith Abraham, even though he was past age—and Sarah herself was barren—was enabled to become a father because he considered him faithful who had made the promise" (Heb. 11:11). Here were two people who had shared the disappointment over the years of being childless. They had no tangible reason to think anything had changed. Yet God gave his word to them. And that word was made good in the birth of Isaac.

If a promise of the Word of God flies in the face of your life circumstances, which seem to be crushing you, take heart. You can lift your eyes and go forward, because God is faithful. Whether made to Abraham, David, Paul, or you, God has never given a promise that he failed to honor.

One of the verses that means the most to me in this connection is 1 John 1:9. "If we confess our sins, he is faithful and just and will forgive us our sins and purify us from all unrighteousness."

It is a common human phenomenon to measure our sense of spiritual security and well-being by the way we feel at a given moment. Thus an unsavory event from the past becomes a matter of public record, and we hang our heads and question our relationship with God. Something bad happens, and we begin to wonder if we are even saved. People become overwhelmed with anxiety and depressed about their spiritual lives. Has God turned his back and rejected us as his children?

The way to judge your relationship to God is not in terms of your feelings at a given moment, which may or may not be a reliable guide, but by God's promises. If you have had the humility and penitence of spirit to confess the sin—whether it is a private matter known only to you or something everyone has learned of—God is faithful. No matter how humiliated you are over it, the only true guide to your relationship with God is not that depressed sense of the embarrassed moment, but God's personal faithfulness to his word. You are forgiven. God is faithful, and he forgives his children who walk before him with contrite hearts.

Often people will need someone to stand close and help them accept in their minds the reality of what a faithful God has already done. They cannot forgive themselves long after God has forgiven them. The problem is not that they have not repented, but that they do not yet understand the reliability of God adequately to really trust him.

God is also faithful in keeping watch over his people. Here are a couple of precious promises from God through two different writers. Watch the use of the word *faithful* in each of them.

> No temptation has seized you except what is common to man. And God is faithful; he will not let you be tempted beyond what you can bear. But when you are tempted, he will also provide a way out so that you can stand up under it (1 Cor. 10:13).

> So then, those who suffer according to God's will should commit themselves to their faithful Creator and continue to do good (1 Peter 4:19).

What is the message of divine faithfulness in times of stress? In any trying situation which would put your hope in jeopardy, God is going to be there to take your part. True to his word, God will never allow the heat to get higher than you can stand; there will always be a way of escape provided for you. So continue doing good, and be faithful to him. He is being faithful to you.

God's faithfulness is personified in Jesus Christ. He came among men making this pledge: "My food is to do the will of him who sent me and to finish his work" (John 4:34). The word *faithful* doesn't appear in that statement, but faithfulness is its theme. Jesus announced that he was here to complete a task, to see it through to the end. Do you remember his words on the cross? "It is finished!" He came with a mission to perform, and he stayed with it to a bitter end—even when it was evident that faithfulness would put him on a cross.

Going to the cross was not only an act of faithfulness to God; it also proved him faithful in his role as High Priest to the people he loves. One New Testament writer explains the incarnation with these words: "For this reason he had to be made like his brothers in every way, in order that he might become a merciful and faithful high priest in service to God, and that he might make atonement for the sins of the people" (Heb. 2:17).

In faithfulness, both to the Father and all those who desired a relationship with the Father, Jesus proved himself utterly dependable. He was "faithful to the one who appointed him" (3:2) in making salvation a reality.

Just as the Father and Son have exhibited such unfailing reliability in all their works, so is the Spirit dependable in his work of empowering believers to a lifestyle of holiness.

Faithfulness as a Christian Virtue

A characteristic feature of the unbeliever (who does not have the Spirit of God within him) is fickleness. He is unable to be consistent in spiritual things. His pronounced inability to be dependable in relation to what he knows to be right and holy relates most directly to the vice of selfishness. When one lives at a worldly level, serving the passions of the sinful nature, he is always looking for greener pastures. Somebody else always has a situation which looks better than his, a love which seems more exciting than his, or possessions which appear more satisfying than his. So, no matter what he attains, he always sees what somebody else has and is envious. He is living at the level of his sinful nature.

Selfish people do not have the ability to be constant, to make commitments and see them through, to handle difficulties. There are just too many diversions along life's course which turn their heads away from primary purposes and trap them in life's snares.

A Christian's movement toward maturity in Christ is measurable largely in terms of progress toward dependability. Throwing off the old instability and fickleness and replacing it with this virtue of faithfulness is an evidence that one is yielding to the presence of God's Spirit in his life.

Faithfulness is only rarely demonstrated in martyrdom; it is usually displayed in the little tasks of life that tend to wear us down. In fact, almost every Christian has had a mountain-peak experience of devotion such that, if he or she had been called on to die for Christ right then, no fierce lion or firing squad could have shaken faith. A much smaller percentage of us can deal with the little things like committee meetings, cranky neighbors, or irritations from the children.

In relation to a local church, generous and consistent giving is an evidence of faithfulness. So is regular attendance at worship assemblies. Participation in ministries is an even better indicator, because that is more demanding than putting money in a plate or reserving a fixed time to assemble for worship. Being called on at awkward hours to serve others in difficult ways requires dependability.

Personal purity in daily living is even more difficult still. Biting your tongue rather than firing back in anger. Refraining from coarse, obscene language when you work among people who use it freely. Learning to return good for evil. Resisting the temptation to jump into a "greener pasture" when you've made a commitment to stay in *this* pasture—this marriage, this business deal, this job assignment. The ability to carry through with responsibility is what faithfulness is about.

In his correspondence with Christians at Corinth, Paul spoke of his apostolic ministry in these words: "Now it is required that those who have been given a trust must prove faithful" (1 Cor. 4:2). Having been called to be an apostle and to be entrusted with divine revelation, his duty was to be dependable for the Lord's purposes. What did that mean for him? Stoning, shipwreck, and beatings. Long, lonely final hours in a dungeon cell. Death.

What does faithfulness mean for some of you reading these lines? Staying in Christian ministry when no one appreciates the sacrifices you make to do so. Living daily with the agony of a birth defect or injury. Staying with a marriage partner who seems intent on breaking your spirit. Loving a rebellious child who seems to go out of his way to find new ways of jabbing daggers into your heart. Learning to deal with a colostomy after cancer surgery. It is human to let go in these tough situations; it is divine to exhibit staying power by the Spirit's enabling.

As one speaker put it, living for Christ is seldom like taking a million-dollar gift from God and returning it all on the altar at any one time. It is more normally cashing in the million-dollar gift for single dollar bills and quarters, then spending $2.75 here and $1 there. Giving all to Christ isn't going out in a blaze of glory, but going on steadily over the long haul.

The late Ray Kroc, the man who built the McDonald's fast-food empire, composed the following statement which was on his office wall:

> Nothing in the world can take the place of persistence.
> Talent will not; nothing is more common than unsuccessful men with great talent.
> Genius will not; unrewarded genius is almost a proverb.
> Education will not; the world is full of educated derelicts.
> Persistence, determination alone are omnipotent.

Warren Bennis and Burt Nanus, *Leaders.* New York:
Harper & Row, 1985, p. 45.

From a Christian point of view, it is not persistence and determination which are omnipotent, but the indwelling Spirit who creates the virtue of dependability in the lives of God's people.

People Who Won't Quit

I admire people who stay with difficult tasks, pay their bills, complete their assignments, keep their appointments, and otherwise honor their commitments. These are the people who hold society together. They are the practical exhibitions of the increasingly rare virtue called *faithfulness* in the Word of God.

It is difficult to imagine why it is so rare. Perhaps parents are at fault for not teaching it to their children. Maybe we have failed to stress this theme in our sermons and Bible classes. Or perhaps the mind-set of this world is simply so hostile to God that a quality rooted deeply in his very nature can only be despised by our generation.

Too many people walk away from their marriage commitments because there are problems. They abort their unborn babies for the sake of a possible defect which might come attached. They turn their backs on their adolescent offspring who have embarrassed them by their involvement with drugs. Some people cannot hold jobs because of their inability to get to work on time or meet their deadlines. Those same folks are useless in local churches, for they cannot be depended on to carry through with responsibilities entrusted to them.

For the sake of telling you his story, I will call him Elmer. We became friends several years ago. On a low-income salary, he and his wife reared two children and gave them a good education. The entire family followed Elmer's example of devotion to the Lord Jesus in everything. Their family involvement with others is responsible for several people becoming Christians.

Elmer did all this in the course of a lifetime filled with disappointment and pain. He and his wife lost a third child, a daughter, when she was only three. He suffered a massive heart attack from which the doctors said he would never recover. Inadequate health insurance left him with thousands of dollars in bills, but he did recover and went back to work.

In spite of his health problems and the financial strain his illness had created for his family, he took in a nephew whose family had kicked him out after a run-in with the law. Then, seven years after his heart attack, he was found to have cancer. Although he suffered tremendously in the last few weeks of his life, nobody ever heard him complain.

When Elmer died, he left a mortgaged house, a pile of medical bills, and a rich legacy of spiritual treasure to all of us who had known him. Thank God for faithful people who won't give up.

Trust *and* Effort

When one confronts this issue of faithfulness directly, the perennial question about faith and works comes to the fore. Is holiness a matter of passive resignation to the Spirit's power? Is holiness a matter of conscious effort on the part of the Christian?

Framing the question as I just have offers you a false dilemma. Holiness to God is *active submission* to the Holy Spirit and *effort based on trust* in Christ's sufficiency to his own. It is not doing *or* believing for Christians, but believing *and* doing.

We *race* (*see* Heb. 12:1), *fight* (*see* Eph. 6:10–18), and *do good deeds* (*see* Titus 3:8). Our incentive, power, and accomplishments come from the Spirit who indwells and enables.

On the one hand, we are assured: "His divine power has given us everything we need for life and godliness" (2 Peter 1:3a). On the other, we are told: "For this very reason, make every effort to add to your faith goodness . . . knowledge . . . self-control . . . perseverance . . . godliness . . . brotherly kindness . . . love" (1:5–7). The Spirit-led apostle who gave these exhortations apparently felt no sense of contradiction between them. Neither should we feel a sense of contradiction in heeding them.

The concept of "active submission" may sound mystical at first. In the final analysis, however, it is the only appropriate way to represent a believer's response to God. The trouble with Old Testament Israel was that it was willing to accept all the privileges involved in a covenant with God without accepting the corresponding responsibility; in approaching God in that fashion, Israel had forfeited the privileges. The nation received a promise through Abraham with eagerness, but the Ten Commandments were given with the expectation of obedience. If circumcision was the symbol of the covenant and Israel's faith in God, obedience should have been the daily response to the commands given through Moses. Israel should have demonstrated active submission to covenantal status.

With New Testament Israel, the church, the basic elements of trust in God's promise and obedience to God's law still go hand in hand. Where the gospel's good news of salvation by grace is received gladly, the practical obligations of that gospel are accepted as well. Where the obedience of active submission is lacking, there is not faith in the biblical sense. It must be more than mere words when we sing:

> Trust and obey,
>   For there's no other way
> To be happy in Jesus,
>   But to trust and obey.

To reject the obligations of the gospel is to forfeit its benefits.

Remember the Parable of the Talents? The man given five talents returned ten, and the man entrusted with two brought back four. Here is the commendation given to each: "Well done, good and faithful servant! You have been faithful with a few things; I will put you in charge of many things" (Matt. 25:21,

23). The servants had been judged trustworthy by their master, and they had demonstrated their loyalty by proving themselves dependable. The servant who had been "wicked and lazy" in handling the one talent given him was rejected and denied his master's reward.

The Lord of heaven and earth needs dependable servants. You and I are the only ones he has! He will not expect us to have the same gifts or great abilities, but he will require faithfulness with whatever gifts and opportunities do come our way. The issue is not the amount of giftedness, but *dependability.*

The Difference It Makes

Copeland Baker, one of the elders of my home congregation, attended the graduation exercises of the Baxter Preacher Training Institute in Tegucigalpa, Honduras, in 1985. When he returned home from that trip, through tears he told me of an evangelist he met there.

Israel Flores was preaching on the public square of a town in northeastern Mexico. The police came and told him, "You will not be permitted to preach in this city." They arrested him and took him off to jail. They threatened him and told him that he would be released the next day, but that he would have to leave the city. They made it clear that no more preaching would be done by Flores.

The next morning when they released him, he told the officers, "If you need to find me, I will be on the square where you arrested me yesterday. And I will be doing what I was doing when you found me then. The people of this city must know about Christ, and I believe it is my duty to try to tell them about the gospel."

Upon his release, he went back to the same square and began to preach. No sooner had he begun than the police came. This time some of them beat and kicked him. They literally dragged him to the jail by the hair of his head, pulling out a great deal of his hair and lacerating his scalp. In jail he was beaten again. One officer told him he would be killed if he ever went back to his preaching post again.

When the police chief heard about Flores, he said with a sneer, "This man must want to be a martyr." He interrogated the evangelist personally. At the end of the interview, the chief confessed his faith in Christ and was baptized later that same day! He then arranged for his Christian brother's release and took him to a little community near the city, where he had influence. He asked the people to listen as Israel Flores told about Jesus in a simple way. Practically the entire group received Christ. Under threat and duress, with your life in jeopardy— that is loyalty to the Lord Jesus.

Christian lives are built around the principle of faithfulness. If some of us were under the threat of being beaten or jailed, we might summon up more courage than we do under our present circumstances. Maybe it is too easy to wear the name of Christ where it is socially respectable to do so.

Young believers demonstrate their dependability in completing homework assignments and taking exams without cheating. Children are trustworthy when they do their part of the household chores without having to be nagged. Adults show faithfulness as a life principle in keeping promises, paying bills, honoring commitments. When any believer exhibits dependability in these basic life relationships, he or she is gaining credibility to speak for Christ and positioning himself or herself for responsibility in the kingdom of God.

The trouble with most of us is that we want the spotlight and the great tasks without "paying our dues" in faithfulness to the little things. We even treat the little things with contempt. It was Jesus who said:

> Whoever can be trusted with very little can also be trusted with much, and whoever is dishonest with very little will also be dishonest with much. So if you have not been trustworthy in handling worldly wealth, who will trust you with true riches? (Luke 16:10, 11).

Dependability is not an isolated phenomenon which relates to particular Christian duties—such as attendance at corporate worship, tithing, or committee responsibilities. It is a life-pervading quality that exhibits itself in everything a Christian does. It is what makes him a better family member, a better employee, a better student. It is the Spirit of God who enables this virtue to surface in you or me.

Conclusion

Before reading on to the next chapter, it would be worthwhile to pause for a time of introspection. Faithfulness, dependability, loyalty to the Lord Jesus—it is a key indicator of the Spirit's presence and your active submission to him. Not a million dollars at once, not martyrdom, not going out in a blaze of glory—that would be easier. A dollar's worth of yourself here and there, consistent, steady at the post—this is the more difficult way that our sinful natures balk at.

Having put your hand to the plow, don't look back or you become unfit for the kingdom of God (Luke 9:62). At the end, be able to say with Paul, "I have fought the good fight, I have finished the race, I have kept the faith" (2 Tim. 4:7). What an epitaph for a life spent in service to the Lord Jesus!

Almost anyone can start well. The real trick is to keep your eyes on the original goal, keep moving toward it, and finish the journey you have already begun.

The fruit of the Spirit is *faithfulness.*

10

Gentleness

A Texas evangelist tells about being in a department store last year during the pre-Christmas rush, where a part-time clerk had been hired for the holidays. He estimated her to be eighteen or nineteen years old, perhaps a freshman home for the holidays and picking up some extra money for gifts and school. She was petite, obviously unsure of herself at her new job, unfamiliar with the computerized cash register in front of her, and very vulnerable at her post. She didn't know where layaway was or directions to the catalog-order department, and her department manager was on break. The young clerk was surrounded by a growing circle of impatient, demanding people, each one wanting her attention simultaneously.

The person confronting her at the moment the preacher walked up was a large, angular woman, stylishly dressed. "You advertised this item on sale, and I'd like to know where it is!" she demanded in a loud voice.

The clerk, biting her lip, said, "Honestly, ma'am, I just don't know. I've only been at this job for two days. I'm sorry. I wish I could help you. If you could just be patient until my manager gets back from break, I'm sure he will help you."

The woman, seeming to sense that she had the girl at a disadvantage, raised her voice even louder as she said, "I don't have time to wait on department heads! When you advertise an item and you work in the store, you ought to know where it is. You ought to be able to tell customers like me, ready to pay good money, where we can find those things!"

The little clerk, with trembling voice and watery eyes, said, "Yes, ma'am, I know that, but I've only been here two days. They just moved me into this department this morning, and I don't know much about it. But if you can just be patient. . . ."

"Patient!" the woman snapped. "Patient! My dear little know-nothing, I marvel at your generation of snotty-nosed, sniveling, quivering-lipped, spineless apologizers. Why, when I was your age, miss, I was already the mother of two children. I hoed, picked, cooked, washed, tended, mended, fixed—and you can't even tell me where the mixing bowls are!"

Feeling guilty that he had watched and listened so long, the preacher decided to interrupt the awkward scene in progress. He stepped up to the clerk, in front of the accusing woman who was abusing her verbally, and said, "Hello, miss," trying to sound friendly and reassuring. The girl burst into tears and ran away from the counter.

Why does it make some people feel superior to strip others of their dignity? I don't doubt that the woman was telling the truth. By the time she was the young clerk's age, she probably had done all those things she said. But that didn't give her the right to shatter the fragile personality of another human being.

Why do some people think it proper to purchase their victories at the expense of someone else's humiliation? People who lack the effective presence of God's Spirit in their lives are missing the beautiful quality of gentleness he builds into Christian character. To the degree that you have ever been the victim of that sort of insensitive, harsh treatment, you know what it is to be in a situation where the Spirit of God is absent.

Some of us who have been given the Spirit of God resist his work at this point. His transforming work is not *over*powering; it is *em*powering. His role is to produce Christ-likeness in us, but he cannot do that against our wills. We have to be submissive and seeking for it to happen.

It goes against the sentiment of our age for people to be gentle with one another. Read the management books about pushing, shoving, getting ahead, and looking out for number one. It doesn't sound very much like gentleness, does it? We have been sold the idea that gentle attitudes and meek behavior are compromising, weak, and unworthy. Gentleness in men is often equated with being sissy or effeminate. The same trait in women is sometimes berated as a concession to conditioning in a sexist culture.

Nowhere is the contradiction between flesh and Spirit more apparent than at the juncture of harshness versus gentleness. Gentle souls are not weak; they are gracious. They are not fighters but lovers. They are not fierce but merciful, because the Spirit of God is in them. Gentle souls refuse to throw their weight around—even when they have influence and power to wield. Instead, they treat other people with courtesy and genuine concern.

Consider the experience of an immature adolescent who thinks it his responsibility to look tough, talk tough, and act tough. This is because he is insecure. Contrast him with a mature adult who abandons that crusty approach for a poured-out, self-giving, gentle lifestyle. He has lived through his insecurities and learned how to live.

The same sort of thing happens in one's spiritual development. When a person feels compelled to talk judgmentally, act threateningly, and throw his weight around in games of church politics, his behavior signifies spiritual immaturity. Maturity comes when a person can be a poured-out, self-giving, gentle soul— when he can consciously make himself vulnerable before others for their sakes.

The Gentleness of Jesus

The gentleness of Jesus is the perfect example. In Matthew 11:29, Jesus said of himself, "I am meek and lowly in heart" (KJV) or "I am gentle and humble in heart" (NIV). Only a person who is strong can exhibit the gentleness which is given by the Spirit of God. The insecure, weak person lashes out at other people to cut them down to his small size. Paranoia in the face of life's challenges produces petty, abusive, and arrogant treatment of other people. Jesus, on the other hand, is the example of what one can do in a strength posture to show gentleness.

What we see in Jesus is so foreign to the expectations most of us would have had if we had been on the cosmic sidelines to witness his entry onto the human stage. We would have expected a good PR firm to pave the way. We would have anticipated a lot of hoopla, with balloons and streamers and ribbons. We might even have added our suggestion for loudspeakers and brass bands. And then and only then would we have expected to see the Son of God march triumphantly to center stage.

How did it happen? How did the Son of God make his appearance?

There was a lonely voice crying in the wilderness. A baby was born to a peasant girl in an animal shelter in a little town. The baby's life was in jeopardy from a jealous old man. It wasn't an auspicious beginning. Any self-respecting public-relations man would have felt himself a failure if he could do no better for a client. His firm would probably fire him for bungling the assignment. But that is how God introduced his Son to the world.

Paul once wrote of the way Christians are supposed to live and relate to one another. In the early verses of Philippians 2, he talked about comforting one another in love and being like-minded in love, rather than acting in selfish and vain ways. He continues:

> Your attitude should be the same as that of Christ Jesus:
>   Who, being in very nature God,
>   did not consider equality with God
>   something to be grasped,
>   but made himself nothing,
>   taking the very nature of a servant,
>   being made in human likeness.
>   And being found in appearance as a man,
>   he humbled himself
>   and became obedient to death—
>   even death on a cross!
>   Therefore God exalted him to the highest place
>   and gave him the name that is above every name,
>   that at the name of Jesus every knee should bow,
>   in heaven and on earth and under the earth,
>   and every tongue confess that Jesus Christ is Lord,
>   to the glory of God and Father (Phil. 2:5-11).

Christ's attitude is the one we ought to have. He didn't hold on to the position and status that were his by right. He turned them loose. He emptied himself of his rights and prerogatives and made himself nothing. Or, as the older translation says, he made himself "of no reputation." It is too easy for us to be status-conscious, from the clothes we wear and the cars we drive to the neighborhoods we choose to live in.

Jesus didn't have a clergy sticker on his car and a special parking place at the church building. He didn't seek pompous titles or wear special robes that would inspire people to give him special treatment.

When Jesus emptied himself, made himself of no reputation, and was obedient, he was not acting from a "strong position"— as the world judges these matters. From the perspective of the pagans, the strong person is the one who tramples on people who are weaker than himself and then sticks out his chest to boast. He expects others to whimper and snivel in his presence. Is that *really* strength? To the contrary, that is a weak person. That is a cowardly, little-souled person. That is an insecure and rotten person.

The Son of Man didn't resort to coercion and intimidation. He never threatened or stepped on people. The fact that he was strong and secure was evidenced in the fact that he refused ever to act that way.

Jesus revealed the Father to struggling, lost people who did not know him. He called people to heaven and left them to choose without coercion.

Remember the Rich Young Ruler? "What must I do to have eternal life?" he asked. Jesus looked into his heart, saw his idolatrous worship of money, and told him he would have to part with it all. His answer? "I can't do that. It is asking too much!" And then he began walking away. Jesus did not chase after him to say, "Now wait a minute! Maybe we can talk this through and come to a mutually acceptable arrangement." He did not manipulate him, twist his arm, or tell him a deathbed story.

Jesus respected the personhood and integrity of people he met. He came among us and represented the Father's will faithfully. He told the truth and left people to make their free and un-manipulated choices.

Contrast that evangelistic method of gentle respect with the carnival atmosphere and strong-arm techniques of some people today. The noble end in view of sharing Christ does not justify the unethical use of tacky and exploitive means. Some of the personal evangelism programs I have seen must have been modeled on the style of a shady used-car salesman. Some of the crusade sermons I have endured were built on emotional stories rather than Scripture. And sometimes the presenter—whether in private or public settings—clouds the issue of choosing Jesus with choosing *us*.

I recall an incident from about a year-and-a-half ago which underscores this point in my mind. A man and I had been studying together for several months. He had no background acquaintance with Christianity, but he was intelligent and had learned the gospel message. He learned of Jesus as we studied one of the Gospels in detail. He knew the meaning of the cross and what that signified to his need for salvation. We were at the point of impasse, and he had to make a choice.

What was so difficult about the situation related to his family. There were tremendous pressures being put on him by his unbelieving parents. He would have to go one way or the other, maintaining old loyalties to his mother and father, or declaring a new one to Jesus.

The scene is still as vivid in my mind as if it occurred yesterday. He and I were sitting on a couch in my home with our Bibles open. He raised his eyes from his reading and looked me in the eye and said, "Rubel, will you and I still be friends if I don't become a Christian?"

Some of us would find it difficult to continue being friendly with somebody if our goal had been simply to be friendly in order to get him to accept the message we teach. But is that the reason for which Christians befriend people? Is that why we clothe children? Is that why we feed hungry people? Or do we do these things genuinely, in the Spirit of Christ, because he has led us to empty ourselves?

To love people and to serve them just because they need love and service is Jesus' method. In the context of our service, the opportunity will present itself to share the gospel—but rejection of the message does not end a Christian servant's duty to that person.

When that question was put to me, it struck me just how perilous it is to be a teacher of the Word of God. Have you ever rejected someone because he rejected your attempt to share Christ? When you do that, you show yourself unworthy of teaching the gospel, because your motivation is not consistent with that of Christ's, as he pointed people to the Father.

"Will I still be your friend?" I repeated. "Our friendship isn't conditional on your accepting what I've been trying to show you or your becoming what I am. I would hope our friendship will continue unmarred, whatever you decide about Christ." He isn't a Christian today, but we are still friends. We still see each other. We still have lunch together occasionally. I still pray that he will become a Christian one day. But he will be my friend whether or not he ever accepts Christ.

There is a fascinating comment in Matthew's Gospel about Jesus and the sort of gentle person he was. It was found in the context of Jesus' healing the sick and doing deeds of kindness to many different people. The situation called to mind a quotation from the Book of Isaiah. The Old Testament passage is about the Suffering Servant of God and the nature that servant would exhibit.

> Here is my servant whom I have chosen,
>   the one I love, in whom I delight;
> I will put my Spirit on him,
>   and he will proclaim justice to the nations.
> He will not quarrel or cry out;
>   no one will hear his voice in the streets.
> A bruised reed he will not break,
>   and a smoldering wick he will not snuff out,
> till he leads justice to victory.
>   In his name the nations will put their hope (Matt. 12:18-21).

Pay attention to the things that came to Matthew's mind as he observed his Master. Verse 19 says he did not "quarrel or cry out." Contrast that with the theological disputes associated with the name of Jesus since his day. He wasn't quarrelsome. He wasn't a thundering, bellicose, intimidating fellow.

Then verse 20 says: "A bruised reed he will not break, and a smoldering wick he will not snuff out." Does the imagery of a bruised reed communicate anything to you? A bruised reed, or a reed that has already been bent once, is very fragile. You have to be very careful with it and hold it in just the right way or you will break it in two. And what about a smoldering wick? Maybe if you think of a match that has burned down

to the end with barely a flame left on the stem, you can capture
the image.

Jesus was so gentle that a bruised reed in his hands would
never be broken. He was so meek that he could nurse back to
a flame the tiniest spark of fire on a smoldering wick. The point
here is not, of course, to tell us about Jesus' hands or breath.
It is to say there are people whose personalities are as fragile
as a bruised reed or whose faith is as close to dying as a smoldering
wick. There are people who—with one more blow of discour-
agement in their lives—will break in half. They will be crushed
never to rise again.

Jesus Christ was the sort of person in whom Matthew saw
no tendency to discourage or oppress people. He did not break
down men and women under a withering blast. He was the
ultimate encourager. The bruised-reed personality was safe with
him, and the smoldering-wick faith could be revived in his
presence. Although he confronted sin mightily and had no
patience with hypocrites, he would bear with wounded and weak
souls gently, until he nurtured them back to their spiritual health.

Moving now from the first to the fourth Gospel, there is another
revealing incident from the Savior's life, which makes a powerful
point about his gentleness. It is set in the context of Jesus' last
few hours with his disciples. We tend to read this troubling
passage in John 13:12–17 for the sake of explaining what it *doesn't*
obligate us to do. We seldom identify what we are supposed
to learn and imitate from it. It is the scene where Jesus gets
up from the Passover table, picks up a bowl of water and a towel,
and starts washing feet.

> When he had finished washing their feet, he put on his clothes
> and returned to his place. "Do you understand what I have done
> for you?" he asked them. "You call me 'Teacher' and 'LORD', and
> rightly so, for that is what I am. Now that I, your LORD and Teacher,
> have washed your feet, you also should wash one another's feet.
> I have set you an example that you should do as I have done
> for you. I tell you the truth, no servant is greater than his master,
> nor is a messenger greater than the one who sent him. Now that
> you know these things, you will be blessed if you do them."

Some people have thought that Jesus was instituting a church
ritual here. I doubt that. Although I have never been part of

a foot-washing service, I certainly wouldn't object to it. But I think I could guarantee this: If people knew ahead of time what was going to happen, there wouldn't be a dirty foot in the house. I wouldn't come with dirty, smelly feet and expose them to you, and I don't think you would either. We would all be too proud for that. We would be humiliated to take off our shoes if our feet were anything but immaculate, with toenails manicured. So, I really doubt that Jesus was instituting a ritual.

What was being advocated was an *attitude*. Jesus said, "Now I want you to go do for others what I have done for you." Gayle Erwin has captured what I believe to be the essence of this order when he writes:

> If it is not literally to wash feet, then what are we to do to fulfill this commandment? One question in response would be, "What things make us feel cleaner and more fit for the Master's table?"
>
> When someone takes the time to listen to me, I feel as if my feet have been washed. When I am complimented, my feet have been washed. When someone shares a joy with me, my feet have been washed. When someone values my ear enough to share a burden or confess, my feet have been washed. There are countless ways to wash feet. We need only to begin to notice where the dirt comes from in our own lives and we can give cleansing to others.
>
> This thought altered my approach to Sunday sermonizing. I began to realize that neatly dressed people seated neatly in rows are not feeling neat inside. Most of them struggle with non-Christian fellow workers, some listen to constant streams of profanity and off-color stories. Many of the women have been propositioned in the past week. Families sit coolly angry and nonconversant. Guilt, real and unreal, hovers over them and strikes deeply at their inner beings.
>
> Shall I flail them with ominous words from a pulpit? Shall I berate them because they live no better? Shall I blame them for a broken heart? No, they, like me, need their feet washed (Gayle D. Erwin. *The Jesus Style.* Waco, TX: Word Books, 1983, pp. 148, 149).

It is foot-washing when we are about the business of gently encouraging one another, so that those of us whose souls feel like bruised reeds or wicks about to go out leave a worship experience or private conversation with a Christ-like person feeling cleaner, stronger, refreshed.

A Forgotten Concept

The concept of being a "gentleman" or "gentlewoman" is inherent in this fruit of the Spirit, *gentleness*. We don't seem to value the idea of gentlemanly or gentlewomanly virtues in our culture anymore. Rudeness has become stock-in-trade. Thoughtlessness is the norm. Some apparently feel it is acceptable to step on other people's feelings with the attitude, "I can't care what others think. I've got to look out for *my* interests."

Rude, abusive, and hurtful behavior cannot become the norm among those who are followers of Jesus. If we are the temple of the Spirit of God, it will be impossible for us to embrace and practice such a lifestyle.

As the Spirit of God teaches us the virtue of gentle and meek behavior, we will become increasingly aware of and sensitive to others. We will be less likely to hurt someone's feelings by thoughtless words or deeds. We can learn to say "thank you" or "I'm sorry" without difficulty. We will master the skill of making others feel good and sense their worth.

There are several biblical concepts which relate to gentleness. One of them is *meekness*. The meek person who is pronounced blessed in Matthew 5:5 is not a weak or weak-willed individual; he is a strong person whose strength is under restraint. Another is *self-control*, which will be studied in chapter 11. Self-control, understood biblically as Spirit-control, is what enables a strong person to be restrained enough to be gentle with others. Finally, *humility* is a virtue which enables a believer to bear with provocation without yielding to the impulse to retaliate, to be gentle enough to turn the other cheek to an insult.

Moses is called the gentlest or meekest of men in Numbers 12:3. But Moses, gentle as he was with those unbelieving children of Israel, could at other times be ablaze with anger. He didn't always keep things in balance, although for the most part he did. He got angry when he had to, yet he could be gentle when people needed to see that side of his nature.

You won't always get the balance right in your life any more than Moses did in his, but the meekness, restraint, and gentleness of Christ must be there. Otherwise your heart will be closed to the truth God seeks to show you. James 1:21b says it is with meekness (or humility, Gk=*prautes*) that we receive truth. This

virtue not only allows you to *receive* truth but also enables
you to *share* it. It will open other people's hearts to the truth
you bear if you let the Spirit of God teach you to be gentle
with them.

Peter counsels Christian women who are married to unbelieving men to win them to Jesus with a "gentle . . . spirit, which
is of great worth in God's sight" (1 Peter 3:4). Don't argue with
your husband. Don't nag him. Without the volatile sparks of excited
words, just win him over by your life. Exhibit a life of gentle
Christian beauty—with courtesy, kindness, and a loving nature.

First Peter 3:15, 16 tells believers to carry our beliefs before
all men that way.

> But in your hearts set apart Christ as LORD. Always be prepared
> to give an answer to everyone who asks you to give the reason
> for the hope that you have. But do this with gentleness and respect,
> keeping a clear conscience, so that those who speak maliciously
> against your good behavior in Christ may be ashamed of their slander.

Gentleness will even open people to correction when we have
to offer that. "Brothers, if someone is caught in a sin, you who
are spiritual should restore him gently . . ." (Gal. 6:1). If you don't
go to that person in Satan's clutches with gentleness, not only
will you not restore him, you may break him. You will likely
drive him away. You will alienate him from the Lord.

So beautiful a virtue is gentleness that it even opens one's
enemies to the possibility of reconciliation. Take up the gauntlet
of challenge, and the possibility of peace is abandoned. Respond
to a grievance out of a gentle, Spirit-controlled temperament,
and that possibility remains.

Jesus taught us to love our enemies and pray for them (Matt.
5:44). He commanded that we learn to turn the other cheek
to insults from evil people (vv. 38, 39). He set a perfect example
in praying for the people who had nailed him to a cross: "Father,
forgive them; for they know not what they are doing" (Luke 23:34).
Against this background, the tendency of our sinful natures to
be always "fighting fire with fire" seems a bit tawdry.

I read in the newspaper a while back of a fence now 16-feet
high between the yards of two men. One blows his horn at 2:00
A.M. to wake the other; the man on the other side dumps garbage

in front of the first man's house, and so on. Each round is an escalation of what went before. It even happens in the church—both in local congregations and in a larger brotherhood. Alienation and division result from charge and countercharge. Failing to live with the good of the body in mind and in love for one another, Christians behave as pagans to "bite and devour" one another (Gal. 5:15).

While Robert E. Lee was a cadet at West Point, a classmate took a violent dislike to him. Over the years, he made repeated attacks on Lee. One day an acquaintance asked Lee what he thought of the man, and he spoke of him in glowing terms.

"You must not know what he has been saying about you for years," the man said.

"You did not ask me what the man thought of me," Lee replied, "but what was my opinion of him."

Christians must live above the pettiness which pits neighbor against neighbor, family member against family member, or Christian against Christian. We must learn to be generous of heart, ignore unkindness, and refuse to answer back. We must allow the Spirit of God to make us into gentle people.

Conclusion

As William Barclay expressed it:

> It is when we have *prautes* that we treat all men with perfect courtesy, that we can rebuke without rancour, that we can argue without intolerance, that we can face the truth without resentment, that we can be angry and yet sin not, that we can be gentle and yet not weak. *Prautes* is the virtue in which our relationships both with ourselves and our fellowmen become perfect and complete (William Barclay. *Flesh and Spirit*. Nashville: Abingdon Press, 1962, p. 121).

Choosing a gentle approach to life by the power of the Holy Spirit allows you to live in peace and security. As God sent the Son to walk gently, meekly, and humbly among men because their souls were hurting, he also sends us.

If the Spirit of God lives in you, you will be less harsh, less arrogant, less provocative. You will be less inclined to throw your weight around, and you will be increasingly humble and gentle.

It probably won't win you any fame. You certainly won't get this world to stand up and applaud you for being meek, because it will probably mistake your meekness for weakness. It will not get you any admiration from the hard-driving power brokers. But it just may win some people to the Savior.

The fruit of the Spirit is *gentleness.*

11

Self-Control

Self-control is the only element of the fruit of the Spirit which
is negative. It points to the restraint of factors that can lead
to the destruction of self-esteem, character, and spiritual life.

Think of all the people in our culture who struggle, for example,
with problems such as overeating or smoking. Because they
cannot practice self-discipline effectively enough to master their
destructive habits, they lose self-esteem. Or think of the angry
husband who—because he cannot control his temper—is
physically abusive to his wife. And there are those frightening
reports in the newspapers daily about fathers and mothers who,
in situations of provocation, do not have enough self-restraint
to refrain from abusing their children. Then there are young
people who are unable to restrain their sexual desires; they
become sexually active in high school or college. Some adults
cannot be faithful to their spouses and become involved in
extramarital affairs because of a lack of self-discipline.

The list of sins of passion could go on and on. But sometimes
the lack of self-control is much more subtle. It surfaces often
with the sentiment of so many people that life has "gotten out
of control" for us.

For example, some people do not manage their handling of
credit, get in debt beyond reasonable hope of being able to pay,

and are forced into bankruptcy. Sometimes our get-it-now society simply lures people into too many commitments made in good faith but not with good judgment. Or maybe it is a matter of overloading a schedule with more activities than any reasonable human being can get into a day or a week and the breaking of someone's emotional stability.

Perhaps it is a mistake to view self-control as a negative feature at all. The only sense in which I see it as negative is that it relates to the restraining of that which can lead us into so many damaging areas.

The word for virtue (Gk, *enkrateia*) is variously translated "temperance" (KJV) or "self-control" (RSV, NIV). It stands opposed to the fornication, impurity, and debauchery, which characterize a life dominated by the sinful nature.

One of the beliefs that frightens me about certain cultic religions is their notion of purity and self-discipline achieved through the abandonment of one human will to another human will. That is not the sort of self-control envisioned in Galatians 5. This form of self-control is a matter of spiritual surrender to the Holy Spirit to the degree that a meaningful internal discipline of a raging and rebellious spirit is realized. In contrast to the cultic monitor who imposes a slavish subservience to a predetermined regimen for its disciples, the monitor who is internal in the form of God's Spirit allows a person to live a life of purity and integrity without slavishness.

As Barclay puts it in his wonderful little book, self-control is:

> that great quality which comes to man when Christ is in his heart, that quality which makes him able to live and walk in the world, and yet to keep his garments unspotted from the world (*Flesh and Spirit*, p. 127).

The Place of Self-Control

Although it is neglected in the list of virtues prized in our time, self-control is both praised and enjoined in Scripture. Take this Old Testament passage as a case in point: "Like a city whose walls are broken down is a man who lacks self-control" (Prov. 25:28).

The image of a city with its walls broken down and breached is clear. It is a place inviting attack and plunder by the enemy.

There is no protection. The city remains constantly vulnerable. The writer says that a person lacking self-control is in the same situation. A human being without self-control is in constant danger of being led to ruin through the blind pursuit of his desires. There are always breaches in the defense. There is constant vulnerability to passions.

There is an interesting reference to this virtue in the New Testament in connection with an event in the life of Paul. Remember his situation after his arrest at Jerusalem? Eventually transferred to Caesarea, the garrison town of Palestine, because of threats made against his life, Paul was placed in the custody of a Roman procurator named Felix. Paul appeared before Felix and his wife, Drusilla, and the record says: "As Paul discoursed on righteousness, self-control and the judgment to come, Felix was afraid and said, 'That's enough for now! You may leave'. . ." (Acts 24:25).

If you know anything about Felix, you understand why Paul chose to speak on self-control and why Felix was not particularly excited about the topic. Tacitus, the Roman historian, paints this word picture of Felix: "He exercised the prerogatives of a king with the spirit of a slave." His lust for power was never satisfied. At the time of his meeting with Paul, Felix had already made three socially motivated marriages. The third of his marriages was to Drusilla, daughter of Herod Agrippa I. She had been placed in a previous marriage by her father when she was in her early teens. The man she married did not have a promising future, so when Felix met her at the tender age of sixteen, Drusilla was lured by him—by his carnal, sensual desire for her, by his wooing, and by her desire to be advanced through a good marriage. She left her husband to become Felix's third wife.

So when Paul appeared before Felix and Drusilla—people unprincipled and ungoverned in their ambition and greed—he talked to them about righteousness, self-control and the judgment to come. Paul spoke to their need, but they were not interested in adjusting their lifestyles to the control of the sovereign will of God.

Anyone who would serve as a shepherd of the flock of God must show himself to be a man who is self-controlled (Titus 1:8). Lest we think that this virtue is required only of leaders, however, it should be observed that self-control is one of the graces counseled for every believer in 2 Peter 1:6. In fact, the latter passage teaches that the lack of self-control will make one "ineffective and unproductive" in spiritual matters (v. 8).

The Difficulty of Self-Control

The virtue of self-control is contrary to our natural desires. We all tend in our spiritual lives to be immature children. We want *what* we want *when* we want it. The idea of postponing the satisfaction of a desire is abhorrent to us. We want it and we want it now! If it is within our power to get it, even if it means someone else must be deprived or hurt, it goes against our natural inclinations to exercise self-discipline.

And self-control is certainly contrary to the spirit of the times. Isn't it something of a spectacle? We follow it in the media. The president makes a televised speech about the need to change some governmental programs that are out of control to the degree that the government now directs grant money to some 66 million Americans. The deficit continues to grow, and we know we're spending ourselves into an impossible situation—a debt so great that we can't even fathom its magnitude. So as the president talks about the need to restrain the growth of the budget and to work toward handling this deficit, everyone says, "Oh, we agree"—*until* some remedial program is proposed that affects us directly.

Once I followed with interest a couple of strong-willed politicians who had been the strongest of presidential supporters. One of them, chairman of the Senate Finance Committee, was an advocate of the president's plan for cutting back some grants until it came to a timber exemption. Timber is the biggest revenue producer in his home state. The other politician could simultaneously propose cutting senators' salaries and engineer a billion-dollar tobacco subsidy: his is the leading tobacco-producing state in the country.

A Gallup poll indicated that by a two-to-one margin there is a general approval in this country for the proposal of tax reductions and deficit reductions. Yet the same poll revealed overwhelming disapproval of the elimination of deductions that a lot of us depend on in order to finance those reductions.

What a terribly inconsistent situation. It pictures on a large scale this problem of our inability to enforce self-discipline. We want things brought under control, but we want it done against the drift of the what's-in-it-for-me spirit that seems to dominate all of us. If I'm going to have to sacrifice and if I'm going to have to restrain, then I'm not so sure I want anything changed. So it is that a Christian is put into the tension between the sinful nature and the Spirit of God. On the one hand, it is our natural inclination and the spirit of the times to want what we want and never to give up anything for the sake of the larger good of the community or another person. Yet from the Spirit of God and from what we understand of the character of Jesus, we know that self-mastery is a virtue. The struggle begins. The pull begins to tear within our beings.

In First Corinthians Paul draws an analogy between the self-disciplined Christian and an athlete. "Do you not know that in a race all the runners run, but only one gets the prize?" he writes. "Run in such a way as to get the prize. Everyone who competes in the games goes into strict training" (9:24–25a). Anyone intending to win an athletic contest knows he must exhibit intense self-discipline. Something may look good to eat, but if it isn't on the diet needed to prepare for his event, there must be enough self-control to refuse it. He may want to go to a party or stay out late, but there's a certain training regimen, a certain discipline of schedule that he is committed to for that athletic contest; he goes home instead and gets his rest.

Paul continues: "They do it to get a crown [of laurel] that will not last; but we do it to get a crown that will last forever" (v. 25b). In the apostle's analogy, we who are striving for a crown that will last also subject ourselves to discipline, to a regimen of self-mastery.

Genuine self-control by God's Spirit includes the whole of a person's life. It is possible for an athlete to be so self-controlled that he can win Wimbledon but so emotionally undisciplined as to throw temper tantrums on the court and curse officials. It is possible for a believer in Christ to be self-disciplined about alcohol but out of control with food or money. It is possible to show mastery for a time through legalism rather than by the Spirit of God.

It is one thing to criticize politicians for a lack of self-discipline in formulating policy or even lazy athletes who don't realize their potential in Olympic competition. It is something else again to let the topic of self-control become intensely personal to our lives.

The Divine Restraint

The Greek view of human nature enjoined self-control via reason. For Socrates, it was one of the principal virtues. Plato saw it as the control of one's sensual desires, which would be achieved by informing the reason. He believed that anyone who knew what was true, genuine, and right would act virtuously as a matter of course. Our common sense denies the thesis. All too often our knowledge of the right is set aside by a more powerful desire for something forbidden or evil. Plato was wrong in holding that self-control arose automatically from knowledge.

Among the Stoics, some of whose representatives Paul encountered in the Areopagus meeting at Athens, self-control was central to their philosophy of a good life. They taught that it was a cruel form of slavery to be tossed about by one's passions, particularly greed, sexual desire, and the desire for food and drink. Thus they developed a doctrine of human freedom predicated on *enkrateia.* One could be truly free, thus truly human, only when he mastered the desires which tend to enslave him to his body. In its more extreme form, Stoicism led individuals not only to vows of poverty and celibacy but to actual abuse of their bodies.

The Jewish community of Essenes living at Qumran at the time of Jesus also stressed the value of self-control. One of the ideals recommended in that group was asceticism. By a commitment to celibacy, communal possessions, and frequent fasting, one could be regarded as spiritually superior to those who married (considered a concession to sexual lust), maintained private property (viewed as selfishness), or ate normal diets (regarded as little short of actual gluttony).

Into this context of spiritual elitism, which identified self-control with an austere, ascetic lifestyle capable of being embraced only by the few, came the Christian religion with its requirement of *enkrateia* for every believer.

The Christian concept of self-control neither makes Plato's mistake nor falls into the shambles of legalistic asceticism. The awareness that one is obligated to practice self-control comes via knowledge, but the power to do so is not regarded as a concomitant to knowledge; Christian self-control sometimes involves denying oneself the same thing an ascetic refuses, but the motive and strength for doing so come from a source larger than inner strength of will.

In the New Testament understanding of self-control, there is no inherent value in this virtue which makes one into a saint. To the contrary, it is a gift of the Spirit to one who is already a saint by virtue of his salvation by grace through faith. It is an evidence of regeneration, new birth, and eternal life in a man or woman.

From the Christian perspective, then, *self*-control is really *Spirit*-control. The virtue translates to the following in practical terms: "I have been crucified with Christ and I no longer live, but Christ lives in me" (Gal. 2:20a). Or, expressed in words only slightly different but with the same meaning: "For to me, to live is Christ" (Phil. 1:21a).

Some Areas to Watch

This matter becomes personal to us only when we start looking at specific issues in our lives. Greek philosophers, senators in Washington, and non-Christian libertines are one thing—but what about the areas where you and I struggle?

Maybe it becomes personal to you in a passage such as this: "A fool gives full vent to his anger, but a wise man keeps himself under control" (Prov. 29:11). What we usually call a *bad temper* is here referred to as "giving vent to anger." This feature of human relationships has already been referred to in relation to the abusive behavior of some husbands and wives toward each other. (Occasionally I've even heard married people defend their abusive tempers and behavior as part of the passion that makes their relationship "colorful." Most of the colors I've seen as a result come in two shades—black and blue—not the sorts of colors that make a marriage beautiful or reveal it as a work of God.) And, oh, what some people do in work relationships or even within the church of God to cause tempers to flare!

Still, the Bible doesn't call us to live as bland, passionless characters who have no ability to be angry. Some subjects ought to make Christians blaze with anger. Direct affronts against the holiness of God, immoralities pushed on us and our children— these ought to cause rage within us. Yet Ephesians 4:26 says,

"In your anger do not sin. . . ." The same verse offers this rule of thumb for the disposition of anger: "Do not let the sun go down while you are still angry."

A passionate side to Christian character causes us to have feelings and the capacity for anger. Jesus did, but he was always able to master his anger against the temptation to strike out to hurt people. He channeled his anger to do something constructive, to make changes for the better.

We are sometimes prone to defend ourselves by pleading, "But you don't understand. That's just the way I am. If you had known my father and my grandfather before him, you'd know it's just within our family. It's something I can't control. Maybe you're not that way, but. . . ."

I think the lamest excuse there is for some of our daily vices is that old plea "It's just the way I am." Now if you tell me that bad temper is part of your natural makeup, I cannot call you a liar and say it is not so. What I deny is that, with the presence of the Spirit of God in your life, there is any justification for your remaining that way. The whole issue of the indwelling Spirit of God has to do with empowering change into the likeness of Jesus.

Maybe the issue in your life is not so much temper as *sexual passion.* In 1 Corinthians 7, Paul discusses a number of questions related to marriage—some of them being problems of controversy that still rage among believers about how to handle certain relationships. What about people who have never married? What about people married to unbelievers? And what about people who are divorced?

Without trying to cover the entire range of issues that Paul raised, there is one in particular that is a constant concern among Christian people, especially among younger Christians. What the apostle says at one point in the chapter confuses some folks: "Now to the unmarried and the widows, I say: It is good for them to stay unmarried, as I am" (1 Cor. 7:8).

Paul was not offering a general counsel against the righteousness or holiness of the married state. That would be inconsistent with everything he says here and in other passages. (Later in the chapter he talks about a crisis situation at Corinth, explaining that forming a marital relationship at that time would be a matter of special stress, and that it would be best to delay marriage until the crisis was passed.) But having given his counsel, he immediately anticipated the situation of some and wrote: "But if they cannot control themselves, they should marry, for it is better to marry than to burn with passion" (v. 9).

Sexual desire is as normal to healthy human beings as the desire for food and drink. It is holy, it is of God, and it is designed to give great joy and satisfaction to people *within the relationship of marriage.* The difficulty comes in the fact that passion does not wait until after the wedding ceremony to make its stirrings felt. Passion arises when someone meets that very special person and love begins to mature out of friendship. And just as it is natural for a person to say, "I love you," and by words and deeds and gifts to express love, it is also natural to want to express that love in the special experience of sexual union.

Those of us who are Christians understand that, as natural and as holy as such a desire is, there must be restraint until such time as that desire can be fulfilled legitimately and with God's approval within the context of marriage. And so young people who are dating or engaged are not only tempted but sometimes yield to the temptation with the excuse that they are truly in love, intend to be married, or have set the wedding day. But what happens in a frighteningly high percentage of those instances is that once the integrity of the two people begins to be compromised, the relationship that caused them to love each other initially begins to break down. A sense of guilt destroys what otherwise was beautiful and could have become even more beautiful. As a general rule, I am against long engagements precisely because of this matter of temptation. If two people are physically, intellectually, and socially mature enough to accept the responsibilities of being married, it is better for them to marry than to burn with passion.

Paul acknowledged that there is a threat to one's ability for self-mastery because of the sexual passions that burn within normal people. And, of course, these passions are sometimes experienced in relationships very different from courtship. After marriage occurs, one is still able to feel passion or to have passion aroused by someone other than his or her mate. At that point, the mastery and discipline of the Spirit of God must become a reality to keep the commitment to keep the marriage holy. It is by his power rather than natural inclinations that one can

forego a clandestine affair of the sort that has ruined so many
lives and that is an affront to the holiness of God.

Maybe the special challenge for another person is that unruly
member of the body, the tongue, that every human being has
to bridle. The Bible acknowledges that nobody can tame the
tongue completely. "No man can tame the tongue. It is a restless
evil, full of deadly poison" (James 3:8). Earlier in the epistle just
quoted, James went so far as to say that anyone who could control
his tongue fully would be a perfect man. How many perfect people
do you know?

The specific temptation for you may be gossip. Gossip tends
to promote a sense of one-upmanship. There is some special sense
of power for you to be able to whisper to someone as a third
party walks by, "Did you know so-and-so about him?" Whatever
sense of power and self-exaltation that gives, it is a nasty and
evil deed.

"But I only relate things that are true!" protests someone. That
makes it even worse, because anything you tell about another
person that would harm him—even if it is true—is something
God would want you to have enough self-discipline to restrain
telling. If something needs to be done about what you know
concerning that person, let it be done between you and that person
for the sake of helping him—not between you and third parties.

What about lies? Christians are supposed to be people in love
with the truth. Jesus is the personification of truth. The Word
of God that we give our devotion to is truth. Paul says in Ephesians
4:25a: "Therefore each of you must put off falsehood and speak
truthfully to his neighbor." We are not to give way to half-truths
or untruths.

Then there is the sort of filthy language Paul refers to in
Colossians 3:8. It may well be the language of the times—whether
in music or in casual vocabulary—but nevertheless the sort of
language that glorifies that which is indecent and shameful. It
is part of the self-mastery the Spirit of God would work in us
to keep our language clean and pure.

One matter that we seldom mention relative to self-discipline
is curiosity about other folks' affairs. It takes a great deal of
self-control not to be nosy at times, to pass by a situation which
is really not our concern, and not to put our eagle beaks in
to pry. The Bible calls such persons "meddlers."

The matter of religious dogmatism also relates to self-control. Christians are a dogmatic people about the issues of clear revelation, which stand out in bold relief on the pages of Scripture. On matters where God has spoken clearly and directly, on ethical principles such as are identified in the Ten Commandments, on the offenses that are direct affronts to the holiness of God—Christians cannot afford to be anything but dogmatic on these matters. God has spoken, and he has spoken clearly.

Sometimes, however, we have to fight the tendency to be dogmatic about everything and to act as if everything on which we have an opinion is a matter which deserves the degree of dogmatism we ought to reserve for God's clearly stated revelation. To be an opinionated, pushy person, always having to have the last word on everything, demonstrates a lack of self-control.

Conclusion

When I was in junior high school, I must have put a million miles on a chrome-fendered Schwinn bicycle my dad bought me. I wore out several tires—always rear tires before the front ones. I remember one day when I was going down a steep grade, feeling more and more exhilarated as my bike picked up speed and made the wind rush by. I saw a curve at the bottom of the hill, but it was just too much fun to be riding at top speed. So I decided I could negotiate that curve without brakes. As a result, my beautiful bike suffered significant damage as I lost control in the curve—and I suffered even more damage.

There are happenings in our lives which feel so good that we are inclined not to put on any brakes. We don't exercise discipline or restraint, even when we know that good judgment—let alone right principle—requires it.

Anything out of control in your life today is still susceptible to the restraining power of the Spirit of God. The call you hear is not an appeal to asceticism; that is an appeal to the flesh, a cultish alternative to Christian self-control, and breeds pride and a condescending attitude. The call you hear is the appeal of the Spirit of God for you to surrender to Jesus; give the right of rule in your life to Christ, and he will return it to you with the authority to reign.

Once you say, "Jesus, I abandon my will to you and will live under your lordship henceforth," he will respond, "Now I will make you a king to reign in my power." Or, to use the language of Romans 5:17, you will begin to "reign in life" with the Lord. By abdicating first place in your life to Jesus, he rewards you with a kingly status and teaches you the mastery of self.

What self-help programs can never achieve in the total discipline of a life is God's gift as an element of his fruitful Spirit.

The fruit of the spirit is *self-control.*

12

"Be Filled with the Spirit"

The church at the end of the twentieth century is something of a sleeping giant. It is a *giant* because of the powerful resources available to the church and the marvelously great and noble ministry it has been given. Yet it is *asleep* because we have lost sight of the importance and urgency of our task.

When I see how little we are doing to evangelize the world, I sense that we have lost our way. With whatever else that is legitimate for the church to be about in the world, our first task is to make known the saving message of Jesus. The original mission given the apostles has fallen to those of us who have believed through their word: "Go into all the world and preach the good news to all creation" (Mark 16:15).

When I see how little we are doing to bandage the wounds of the world, I sense that we have lost our way. One of the appealing things about Jesus, which caused people to consider his bold claims to deity, was his compassion. Jesus "went around doing good and healing all who were under the power of the devil" (Acts 10:38b). The major moves being taken today to feed the hungry, house the homeless, and heal the sick, are by government agencies and celebrity humanitarians rather than the church of God.

161

We have spent too much of our time and energy on infighting, church politics, and other similar concessions to the sinful nature. There are signs, however, that the sleeping giant is becoming restless. It may yet be roused to activity which is Christ-centered and redemptive.

Something is needed. A lot of young people are bailing out on the church. I can't vouch for their reliability, but the statistics I've heard quoted over the past ten years indicate that half of our own children do not remain in the church when they reach twenty-one. Purity of lifestyle is too often indistinguishable between the nominal Christian and an average good citizen. The impact we are having on the world is certainly less than it should be.

How Do You Awaken a Sleeping Giant?

To speak of the church as a sleeping giant and to point to the need of deeper Christian commitment is not intended as a harsh judgment. Rather, it expresses a fervent dream. I would like to see the church having the same effect in the world it had in the first Christian century. Those earliest Christians turned their world upside down. We've hardly made a dent in ours.

That stimulation—perhaps even *provocation*—is a periodic need in the body of Christ stands attested by the New Testament epistles. Those ancient letters were written to correct aberrant faith and practice. They were designed to light fires under lethargic believers. They were meant to renew vision among discouraged disciples and to call them back to their early enthusiasm for the faith.

In calling the Christians of Asia Minor to a lifestyle appropriate to their faith, Paul spoke out against the "fruitless deeds of darkness" (Eph. 4:11) and called on them to "make the most of every opportunity" (v. 16) in an evil time. He wrote:

This is why it is said:

"Wake up, O sleeper,
  rise from the dead,
and Christ will shine on you" (Eph. 5:14b).

If Paul needed to awaken some first-generation followers of Christ, how can we pretend to be surprised that some of us need to be aroused in our time?

Power in the body of Christ will come from only one source: the Holy Spirit of God. If the people of God are awakened from sleep and put about our mission, we must learn to rely again on the presence and power of the Spirit. Spiritual battles cannot be won with carnal weapons. We can never do the things we are supposed to be doing as the church by reliance on gimmicks, management techniques from the business world, or carnival-atmosphere worship services which entertain but provide no substance for Monday morning's challenge.

The only way we can be what God wants us to be and do what he needs done in the world is to be more filled with and submissive to the Holy Spirit in our lives. As one writer expressed it: "It's not just *residency* of the Spirit which must be established; it's *presidency*." The point of this play on words is deeper than you might realize at first. It is not enough that we acknowledge that the Spirit of God dwells in the children of heaven; we must give him leave to reign within us, to change us, to transform us.

Power can be unleashed in an explosion or it can be harnessed for long-term use. The energy in ten gallons of gasoline, for example, can be released explosively by just tossing a lighted match in its direction. Or that same amount of energy can be channeled into a fuel-efficient internal combustion engine and transport someone five hundred miles. There may be occasional instances where the best use of gasoline is to explode it for the sake of a spectacular but brief outcome, but the general rule would seem to dictate the wisdom of reserving most of it for propulsion through engines. Explosions are spectacular, but controlled burns generate power for the long haul.

Pentecost displayed the power of the Holy Spirit, the likes of which had never been seen before and has not been witnessed since. The Spirit was poured forth in fulfillment of Old Testament prophecy. There were sights, sounds, and supernatural wonders. And that great explosion of power heralded the birth of the church.

But the Spirit of God also works through the church in a "controlled burn"—a disciplined use of his power that transforms lives, empowers service, and exalts Jesus. Just as our physical bodies sustain life by a constant supply of air (Gk, *pneuma*), so the spiritual body of Christ, the church, sustains its life by a constant supply of the Spirit (Gk, *pneuma*).

The daily work of the church does not exhibit the sparkle and drama of Pentecost, with its tongues of fire and supernatural signs, in every generation. Its worship, fellowship, and outreach are empowered by the measured flow of his incessant energy through the church.

No Law Against These Things

There is no command in Scripture that obligates every believer to be baptized in the Holy Spirit. Baptism in the Spirit was always the result of a promise being fulfilled by God, rather than a command being obeyed by men. There *is* a command, however, that every Christian is to be filled with the Holy Spirit.

On the heels of his comment about awakening sleepers, which has already been cited, Paul added this exhortation: "Do not get drunk on wine, which leads to debauchery. Instead, *be filled with the Spirit*" (Eph. 5:18, italics added). Some Christians are inclined to go light on the first part of this verse. They no longer adopt the historic position of Scripture and the church toward the destructive use of alcoholic beverages. Fewer still take the second part of the verse as worthy of emphasis.

"Be filled with the Spirit" is a hortatory statement in God-breathed Scripture. It is a *command*. To live a Spirit-filled life is not an option if we are to be faithful to our God. If a Spirit-filled life is not Pentecost over again in every generation, then what is it?

A Spirit-filled life is one that exhibits his abiding presence in daily spiritual fruitfulness.

Take one final look with me at the text which has been central to this book:

> But the fruit of the Spirit is love, joy, peace, patience, kindness, goodness, faithfulness, gentleness and self-control. Against such things there is no law. Those who belong to Christ Jesus have crucified the sinful nature with its passions and desires. Since we live by the Spirit, let us keep in step with the Spirit. Let us not become conceited, provoking and envying each other (Gal. 5:22-26).

There almost has to be a touch of irony in what Paul says at verse 23b: "Against such things there is no law." Do we look to the law to show us what is forbidden? Do we commonly use the law to identify for us the evil that we must avoid, sins which are against the will of God that must be eliminated from our lives?

"Search divine law as thoroughly as you will," Paul says, "and you will find no period in history when God ever gave a prohibition against these things: love, joy, peace, patience, kindness, goodness, faithfulness, gentleness, self-control."

God is always found to encourage *love* among his creatures. It is the ability to move outside yourself to seek the good of others, at sacrifice to yourself if necessary.

Joy is an inner satisfaction and sense of delight that comes to you in the knowledge of a secure relationship with God.

Peace is the ability to live in serenity with God, self, and other people in your world. This, too, is God's gift.

Patience is the power to bear with people and circumstances until God brings his own good purposes to light in them. It is a rare quality, but it is certainly not forbidden or unlawful.

Kindness is a willingness to be involved in another person's needs in order to help meet them.

Goodness is upright and honorable conduct which has been tempered by generosity and a charitable spirit.

Faithfulness is the quality of utter dependability, reliability, and loyalty.

Gentleness is strength under divine control. Far from being weak, gentleness is being under harness to God so that the strength of your personality and temperament accomplish his ends.

Then there is *self-control*, the power to restrain the forces and appetites that could enslave, harm, or ruin you.

There is nothing about these qualities—whether considered individually or collectively—that would forbid them to us. So why aren't we more deliberate about nurturing their development? Why are we not more prayerful that God will build these beautiful traits into our lives? Why aren't we more yielded to the Spirit of God so that love, patience, gentleness, self-control, and the like can show through in all we do?

Christians have been bought with a price. Why, then, should any of us continue living to the sinful nature and retain vestiges of the old, unregenerate lifestyle? There is a law against the old ways. It is only life as God's new creation which is free from law's censure and penalty.

In verses 24–26, three final points are made about life in the Spirit, which must be emphasized. Look at each in its turn.

The Sinful Nature Is Crucified

First, all who belong to Christ "have crucified their sinful nature with its passions and desires."

What Paul calls the "sinful nature" ("flesh," KJV) is not the physical body or even its natural desires. It is human personality as stained with and dominated by sin. It is everything evil that man has become and is capable of doing apart from God. It is the old, preconversion man or woman whose heart is focused on the wrong things and whose life is filled with self-willed and sinful habits.

The Book of Galatians calls attention to the constant struggle that goes on between the sinful nature and the Holy Spirit. The sinful nature is not something we inherit genetically, like eye or skin color. It is the learned lifestyle we have developed by imitating the world and resisting the will of God.

When we came to Christ, we repented of the sinful nature's sexual immorality, impurity, hatred, selfish ambition, and other related evils. It is a part of the process of conversion to express not only regret for the ways of the former life but a determination to turn from them. And the living out of the implications of repentance continues daily in the new life of a Christian.

Repentance is not something you do only at the point of conversion. You continue the practice daily as you come to understand the will of God better, as you see images in yourself that are inconsistent with divine holiness, but which were not seen to be so at the time when you became a child of God. Repentance is for the Christian what voting used to be for some people: do it early, and do it often! There will be those occasional times of weakness and lapses of faith which cause you to go back to some of the old, sinful ways temporarily.

Whenever a Christ-follower realizes that his life falls short of his Leader's example, he must renew his change of heart and life. As Paul expressed it in Romans 12:2b, Christian commitment is maintained "by the renewing of your mind"—the *renewing* of your mind rather than the abrupt *changing* as at the start of this experience.

The renewing of a disciple's mind is likely best understood to be the outworking of the repentance which first brought him to know the Lord. He reoriented the total direction of his life in order to become God's child; in his new life there will be periodic times when he renews his commitment; reidentifies the areas of weakness to be prayed about and struggled with; and recommits himself to pursue the goals which are consistent with God's purpose for his life.

Although the old man has been crucified, he struggles to get down off the cross and resume his control over us.

The first requirement of a Spirit-filled life, then, *is daily awareness of human weakness and vulnerability to sin; daily renewal of commitment to the Lordship of Jesus; daily repentance relative to the passions and desires of the sinful nature.*

Marching to a New Cadence

Second, all who live spiritually "keep in step with the Spirit." This is a military metaphor. To "keep in step" is to hold ranks, walk in step with an identifiable leader. The same verb is used in Romans 4:12 of those who walk in the footsteps of Abraham's faith. It carries the connotation in both passages of following a trail someone else has marked for you.

In order for an army to march, somebody has to call cadence for the group. One and only one person will have to be identified to call cadence, or there will be pandemonium. In the new life we have embraced, Christ is our leader. But the Spirit of God calls the cadence, and we keep in step.

I saw something in a Tennessee-Ole Miss football game last year that I had never seen before. From my TV perspective, it appeared that the offensive line of Tennessee had moved early. In fact, at least three guys in orange jerseys moved across the line of scrimmage. Out came a penalty flag, and I thought I knew what was about to happen: the offense would be penalized five yards. As it turned out, I was wrong—again.

When the flag was picked up, the referee explained that the penalty was against Ole Miss. The defense was penalized five yards for "calling false cadence." With the offensive team's quarterback barking signals, somebody on the defensive line had imitated his voice and fooled at least three men on Tennessee's team.

Some of us jump across the line that separates the kingdom of light from the kingdom of darkness because we listen to somebody on the other team call cadence! Unlike in football, however, the penalty is against us. When we are drawn offside, pulled into the world by listening to false cadence, distracted from the Spirit's leading by listening to the siren call of the world— the penalty goes against a Christian's reputation. It can mean the disruption of one's family. It can demoralize a whole church.

To live in submission to the Spirit of God and to walk in step with the Spirit's cadence is not a cowardly lifestyle but a courageous one. It's hard to be a Christian. Especially at the beginning, that which feels most comfortable and natural is that which grieves the Spirit; it is hard to forget such actions and thoughts and leave them to the past. And the disciplines of prayer, fellowship, and unselfish service to others feel strange and unfamiliar; it is difficult to see their value in those early days and to embrace them.

Being a Christian is not like falling off a log. It is the most difficult and demanding life one can be called to live. And that is precisely why the presence of the Holy Spirit is given to each believer when he or she becomes a Christian. It is impossible to live the high and holy life of a child of God by the strengths and abilities of the flesh. If God is not personally present to provide power for the experience, it will end in failure.

In order to live the Christian life, you *have to march to the cadence of the Spirit of God.*

Avoiding Self-Assertion and Pride

Third, people who are living to the Spirit *must "not become conceited, provoking and envying one another."*

Just as it is wrong to live to the flesh by committing fornication or getting drunk, it is also wrong to become arrogant and conceited in the success God gives you in the new life. Suppose you have overcome sensuality or alcoholism. Do you have the right to boast about your victory? One of the snares Satan will use to catch some of us with most easily is our pride.

A sense of satisfaction in overcoming this or accomplishing that may soon become the belief that one is better than the person who hasn't overcome the same vice or spiritually superior to the individual who hasn't accomplished as much. If you have gained a victory in Christ, it is because of the Spirit's power rather than your efforts! So no strutting or bragging is called for, unless you wish to take credit for something you did not do and make yourself vulnerable to pride.

One person's boasting may become another's provocation. Thus, in a context of envious rivalry, people begin comparing accomplishments. Some even exaggerate their conversion experience. Churches compete with each other for the prestige of size and buildings.

Do you remember Jesus' warning in the Sermon on the Mount against calling attention to your spirituality? He wasn't trying to discourage holy actions of prayer and giving to the poor. The warning was against pride in doing them.

> Be careful not to do your "acts of righteousness" before men, to be seen by them. If you do, you will have no reward from your Father in heaven. So when you give to the needy, do not announce it with trumpets, as the hypocrites do in the synagogues and on the streets, to be honored by men. . . . when you pray, do not be like the hypocrites, for they love to pray standing in the synagogues and on the street corners to be seen by men. . . . And when you pray, do not keep on babbling like pagans, for they think they will be heard because of their many words. . . . When you fast, do not look somber as the hypocrites do, for they disfigure their faces to show men they are fasting (Matt. 6:1-2, 5, 7, 16).

When was the last time you mailed an anonymous twenty dollars to a needy family? How long did you pray the last time you were called on to lead the Sunday-school class or worship assembly in prayer? Did you babble any of the standard prayer cliches to pad the prayer? Have you ever fasted without being asked to and without somehow calling attention to it?

The basic point in all these bits of counsel seems to be the same: Let your righteousness be personal between you and God, rather than a matter of public display. Don't call attention to yourself but to the one you serve.

If we are not careful, we can be proud of the fact that we are religious. When that happens, the legitimate testimony to the power of God in our lives trails off into conceit and boasting about our own goodness. Conceit and provocation and envy prove that one is working in the power of the sinful nature, rather than in the strength of the Spirit.

Paul could stand before Felix, Agrippa, and others in the Acts narrative and testify to what God had done in his life. The difference in his testimony and doing what Jesus condemned in the Sermon on the Mount is the difference in revealing what God had accomplished in a sinner's life in order to praise God (and let other sinners realize that the same power can work in them) versus calling attention to oneself in order to gain status in the eyes of men who hear the story. "Let him who boasts boast in the LORD" is still the rule for believers to follow (1 Cor. 1:31; *see also* Jer. 9:24).

I am more than a little suspicious of spiritual-growth programs which rank people by chapters read, visits made, or prospects led to Christ. The statistics about a church's growth rate or baptisms last year may be charted or tabulated for the Lord's glory, but I suspect they are sometimes published for the sake of self-exaltation. Individuals and churches can become competitive in the name of Jesus. But no matter how you sugarcoat such competition to make it palatable to human observers, it must still be ugly to the Lord.

Spiritual Goals by Spiritual Means

So Paul, in effect, says, "I want you to be filled with the Spirit. Remember that your old self has been crucified; don't let him down from the cross. Keep in mind that your life must now be in step with heaven's cadence rather than the world's. And as you begin to see change and transformation in your life, give the glory to God and resist the temptation to brag about yourself. The changes are the Spirit's doings in your life, his fruitful witness to God's power at work in you."

Is such a challenge too great for anyone to accept today?

The time has come for us to be theologically mature enough to approach the doctrine of the Holy Spirit as something other than a battleground. We can be full-blown trinitarians without having to embrace what some of us regard as excesses and false doctrines about the Holy Spirit. We can embrace a healthy and balanced view of the Spirit of God, which allows us to realize that our hope for winning the present struggle is in his power and not in ourselves.

The frustration that we sometimes feel because we haven't achieved our "spiritual goals" is most often a perverse anguish that we have not yet learned how to mobilize the powers and techniques of the flesh, so as to enable us to be what God calls Spirit-led people to be!

Conclusion

When, in 1985, General Motors announced its plan to locate a plant to employ possibly 14,000 workers in a little Tennessee town of 1,094 souls near Nashville, it spawned a new street-corner game. The name of the game was "Spring Hill Property Ownership." It began with someone saying, "Man, don't you wish you owned X acres of Maury County farmland!" The game progressed as you filled in the X with a number, calculated the increase of value your land experienced in the last 30 days, and explained what you would do with the money you could get for selling it. Why, even the most worthless pieces of land in the area became valuable.

We human beings sometimes judge ourselves and others to be "worthless." It isn't really true, for everyone has an intrinsic value by virtue of being made in the image of God. Yet some of us fall so far away from him, mar his likeness in us so terribly, and cover our worth with such disgraceful deeds that we actually become spiritually bankrupt and worthless.

Want to know what to do to change things? Want to raise your worth as a person faster than Spring Hill property values? It's simple. Use the same technique that worked for Spring Hill. Let someone move in whose net worth is so great that his mere presence boosts your value from zero to infinity!

The Lord Jesus cleanses sinners by his blood. And in the same process which saves a man or woman, the Holy Spirit is presented as heaven's gift to indwell the redeemed soul.

Paul tried to call young Christians at Corinth to holiness and Christian purity. Part of their problem appears to have been that they saw themselves as worthless because of their past lives of sin, and despaired of ever doing better. Know what Paul did? He told them they were not worthless, for God's Spirit was using their very bodies as his temple! (1 Cor. 6:14–20). Paul believed a healthy sense of their spiritual worth and the resulting self-esteem they would feel could make them live differently. That awareness still produces the same marvelous effect.

God has a better deal for you than land ownership in Spring Hill. Its value won't fluctuate with the ups and downs of the real estate market. You can be filled to the rim—with him.